Natural Wonders of CONNECTICUT & RHODE ISLAND

— SECOND EDITION —

Exploring Wild and Scenic Places

CAROL HENSHAW

COUNTRY ROADS PRESS

NTC/Contemporary Publishing Group

Library of Congress Cataloging-in-Publication Data

Henshaw, Carol Fairfield, 1931–
    Natural wonders of Connecticut & Rhode Island : exploring wild and
scenic places / Carol Henshaw. — 2nd ed.
        p. cm. — (Natural Wonders)
    Includes bibliographical references (p.) and index.
    ISBN 0-658-00240-6
        1. Connecticut—Guidebooks.   2. Natural history—Connecticut—
Guidebooks.   3. Natural areas—Connecticut—Guidebooks.   4. Parks—
Connecticut—Guidebooks.   5. Botanical gardens—Connecticut—
Guidebooks.   6. Rhode Island—Guidebooks.   7. Natural history—
Rhode Island—Guidebooks.   10. Botanical gardens—Rhode Island—
Guidebooks.   I. Title: Natural wonders of Connecticut and Rhode Island.
II. Title.
F92.3.H465   2000
917.4504'43—dc21   99-047855
                                                                                   CIP

Cover and interior design by Nick Panos
Cover photograph: Atlantic coastline in Newport. Copyright © James
Schwabel/Panoramic Images
Interior illustrations and map copyright © Gigi Bayliss
Spot illustrations copyright © Barbara Kelley
Picture research by Jill Birschbach

Published by Country Roads Press
A division of NTC/Contemporary Publishing Group, Inc.
4255 West Touhy Avenue, Lincolnwood (Chicago), Illinois 60712-1975 U.S.A.
Copyright © 2000, 1995 by Carol F. Henshaw
Printed in the United States of America
International Standard Book Number: 0-658-00240-6
    01 02 03 04 05 ML 19 18 17 16 15 14 13 12 11 10 9 8 7 6 5 4 3 2

To the memory of my parents,
Maxine Fairfield and Herbert Edward Henshaw,
who first introduced me to the beauty and
wonders of the natural world, and
to all those who love the land and its wildlife.

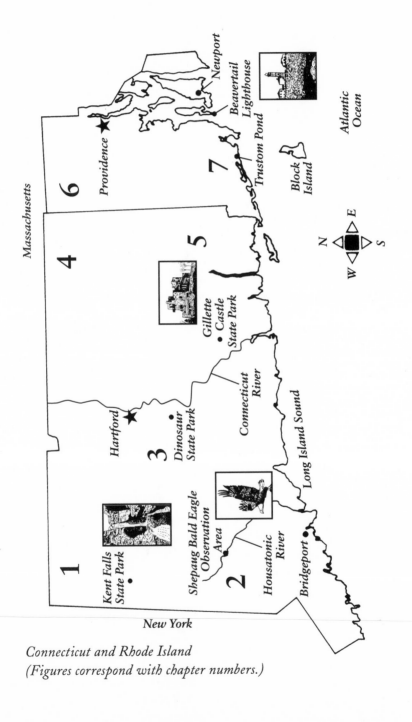

Connecticut and Rhode Island
(Figures correspond with chapter numbers.)

Massachusetts

New York

Atlantic Ocean

Long Island Sound

Providence

Newport

Beavertail Lighthouse

Trustom Pond

Block Island

Hartford

Dinosaur State Park

Gillette Castle State Park

Connecticut River

Kent Falls State Park

Shepaug Bald Eagle Observation Area

Housatonic River

Bridgeport

1 2 3 4 5 6 7

N E S W

Contents

RHODE ISLAND

Acknowledgments

I wish to thank all those persons who have helped in the gathering of information and the writing of this book. It was while I was doing research for the first edition that I first "discovered" the Ansonia Nature and Recreation Center, and subsequently became a volunteer there. I am especially grateful to Donna Lindgren, executive director, at the center, not only for her support and help with this second edition, but for the many opportunities she has provided for new learning experiences both at the center and in the field, related to Connecticut's wildlife, plants, and issues affecting the environment.

I also want to thank Milly Bohannah, instructor of English at the University of New Haven, and my good friend since college days, who not only did the word processing for the first edition, but also edited the text and provided moral support when needed.

I wish to thank John Florian, former editorial director of *Northeast Outdoors*, the publication that first gave me an opportunity to write about camping, travel, and nature-related subjects in the Northeast. Some of the material included in the entries on Kent Falls, Lake Waramaug, Squantz Pond, and Devil's Hopyard State Parks in Connecticut and Beavertail State Park and Conanicut Island in Rhode Island originally appeared in the pages of *Northeast Outdoors*, which until 1996 was published in Waterbury, Connecticut.

I am also indebted to the personnel of the Connecticut State Parks Division of the Department of Environmental Protection, the Division of Parks and Recreation of the

Rhode Island Department of Environmental Management, the Sharon Audubon Center, Flanders Nature Center, and the Audubon Society of Rhode Island for answering questions and furnishing informative material.

Grateful acknowledgment is made to Alfred A. Knopf, Inc., for permission to quote passages from *Reflections from the North Country* by Sigurd F. Olson, published by Alfred A. Knopf, Inc., a division of Random House, Inc., New York, copyright 1976.

Grateful acknowledgment is also made to Rutherford W. Witthus, curator of Literary and Natural History Collections, Thomas J. Dodd Research Center, University of Connecticut Libraries, for extending permission on behalf of the University of Connecticut Libraries to quote passages from *A Naturalist Buys an Old Farm* by Edwin Way Teale, copyright 1974 by Edwin Way Teale, published by Dodd, Mead & Company, New York, 1974.

The passage on page 1 is reprinted from *At the North of Bearcamp Water* by Frank Bolles, copyright 1893 by Frank Bolles, published by Houghton, Mifflin and Co., and the Riverside Press, Cambridge, 1896.

The lines quoted on page 153 are from a book copyright © 1938 by the Regents of the University of Minnesota, reprinted from *Canoe Country* by Florence Page Jaques, illustrated by Francis Lee Jaques, published by the University of Minnesota Press, 1947.

Special thanks go to Jeff Greenwood, director of education at the White Memorial Foundation and Conservation Center, who answered questions and provided me with information on the species of birds, wildflowers, and mammals one might see on White Memorial Foundation lands for both editions of this guide, and to Joan Barry, director of administration and development, for reading and reviewing for accuracy the entry for the second edition.

I am indebted to Roger Lawson, Lead Program specialist, for the Kellogg Environmental Center, for taking time from a busy schedule to read and check for errors the entry on Osbornedale State Park and the Kellogg Environmental Center.

I also wish to express my appreciation to Sherman Kent, president of the Connecticut Audubon Society, and Gail Even, office manager at the Hartford Center of the Connecticut Audubon Society, for their assistance with the first edition.

Finally, I am grateful to Richard Fyffe who in 1994 was humanities bibliographer and curator of literary archives at the Homer Babbidge Library, for his assistance with the entry on Trail Wood, the Edwin Way Teale Memorial Sanctuary.

You all helped to make this book possible.

Introduction

Without love of the land,
conservation lacks meaning and purpose,
for only in a deep and inherent feeling for the land
can there be dedication in preserving it.

—SIGURD F. OLSON
Reflections from the North Country

This is a book about special places in Connecticut and Rhode Island—wonderful parks, nature centers, and wildlife refuges—that exist today, safe from the ravages of commercial development, because of those who so loved the land that they worked hard and fought political battles to ensure its preservation.

In Connecticut and Rhode Island, state and private organizations continue the struggle to preserve our natural environment and to restore coastal and inland bodies of water and streams that have been polluted by those who were more motivated by greed than by a love of the land.

Extraordinary individuals have devoted their lives to ensuring the preservation of land for future generations of men and wildlife. Connecticut is deeply indebted to two residents of Litchfield, Alain C. White and his sister May, who in 1908 set out to preserve the beauty of Bantam Lake and the surrounding countryside for the public to enjoy. Today, the White Memorial Foundation and Conservation Center in Litchfield manages some 4,000 acres. Two outstanding state parks, Kent

Falls and Macedonia Brook, were also gifts of the foundation set up by the Whites.

Probably the most difficult task in writing this guide was selecting the parks and wildlife refuges to be included. I have chosen my favorite destinations, but there are many special places in both states, and some, regrettably, had to be left out. This new edition has five new entries, including two zoos, one in Connecticut and one in Rhode Island. Both are good examples of modern zoos, where the focus has changed from providing entertainment to a concern with education and conservation.

It is with a sense of gratitude that I include the lower Naugatuck River, a river that was once so badly polluted that it was devoid of life, and today is considered one of the best birding rivers in Connecticut. Additional natural areas of special interest may be found in the preserves of The Nature Conservancy. For a guide to these areas in Connecticut, refer to *Country Walks in Connecticut: A Guide to The Nature Conservancy Preserves* by Susan D. Cooley.

The entries are, in general, arranged geographically from north to south and from west to east. They are a guide to some of the best places for nature walks, bird-watching, hiking, canoeing, cross-country skiing, and nature photography. You'll also find special places to swim, camp, or enjoy a picnic.

Whether you visit a state park or a private nature center, it is important to remember that loving the land means leaving no litter behind and not disturbing any plants or animals you find there. A policy of "carry out what you carry in" has been instituted in all Connecticut state parks, which now have recycling stations where you deposit glass, cans, plastic items, and trash in separate bins.

Some Words of Caution

Hiking in both Connecticut and Rhode Island requires a few precautions. Because of the incidence of rabies in wild animals, you are advised not to approach raccoons, skunks, or foxes, especially if the animal appears to be sick or is behaving in a strange manner.

In addition, it is wise to protect yourself against being bitten by deer ticks, which can carry Lyme disease. Ticks are most prevalent in May, June, and July. When hiking in wooded or brushy areas, wearing light colors helps you spot any ticks that attach themselves to your clothing. Hikers are also advised to wear hats, long pants, and shirts, and to tuck pant legs into socks or boots and shirts into pants. On a very hot summer day, you may prefer just to check your skin for ticks after the hike or to use insect repellent containing deet.

All the places included in this guide are relatively safe areas to be in. However, when visiting parks that are easily accessible from large urban areas, you should use the same caution that you would use in a city and avoid hiking alone in isolated areas.

Because water conditions in rivers and streams can change rapidly, it is always wise to scout a stream or to check with local authorities before embarking on a canoe trip.

CONNECTICUT

1

The Litchfield Hills

To the area that is now the town of Kent in northwestern Connecticut, the local Indians gave the name The Place Beyond the Mountains. The Litchfield Hills are the foothills of the Berkshires. While their altitude would not impress anyone familiar with mountains (Mount Frissell at 2,380 feet is the highest point in Connecticut), these rugged hills have a special beauty that draws you back again and again to this part of the state.

Within the boundaries of Kent, 4,000 acres have been preserved as state parks and public lands, including Lake Waramaug State Park, Macedonia Brook State Park, and Kent Falls State Park.

This is the region where you will find hills to climb, deep ravines, romantic waterfalls, sparkling streams, alpine lakes, and deep, cool forests of hemlock, beech, maple, and hickory. Here the Appalachian Trail passes through the state, and the Housatonic River flows between the hills, passing under a historic covered bridge (Bulls Bridge) in Kent.

In Litchfield, you can explore the trails of the state's largest wildlife refuge at the White Memorial Foundation and Conservation Center.

This part of Connecticut is special at any time of year. In winter, it often has snow when the ground is bare in other parts of the state. You can get out and see wildlife, or at least find their tracks, by taking to the trails on cross-country skis or snowshoes. In spring, when the hills are clad in delicate shades of green, you may come to see the cascading waterfall in Kent Falls State Park, observe wildflowers in bloom, or bird-watch at a time when great flocks are migrating north through the valleys.

Summer is a time for swimming and picnics, but it is perhaps in fall that the Litchfield Hills are most memorable. Most years, the display of autumn foliage in northwestern Connecticut is the equal of any in New England, beginning with September's golden days, when purple asters and goldenrod bloom beside country roads, and reaching a climax in mid-October, when the brilliant red maples and golden beech and hickories stand out against the deep green of the hemlocks. Then the hills are covered with a rich tapestry of colors that are reflected in the mirror surface of each pond and lake.

Sharon Audubon Center

At the Sharon Audubon Center (also known as Audubon in Sharon), old stone walls speak of the land's early use for farming, for "Bog Meadow Farm," the home of the Clement Ford family, was once a dairy farm and the biggest producer of golden guernsey milk in New England. The family's gift to the National Audubon Society has assured the preservation of this irreplaceable land for future generations of wildlife, plants, and people.

Today, the center's 754 acres offer a rich and varied environment for wildlife— fields, woodlands, two ponds (one with an observation boardwalk), streams, and marshes that are home to many species of birds and mammals such as beaver, otter, mink, red and gray foxes, deer, bobcats, squirrels, and rabbits. The center also maintains a wildflower garden, herb and vegetable gardens, a butterfly/hummingbird garden, and a wildlife habitat garden that serves as a model for enhancing the wildlife habitat value of small plots of land such as a residential backyard. By providing food, water, and cover for wildlife, you can play an active role in helping to restore the natural ecosystem.

In the main building, you will find a bookstore and gift shop, a museum, the Hal Borland Room, and a children's "Adventure Center." The museum's exhibits focus on the birds, mammals, insects, and amphibians and reptiles native to Connecticut.

The Hal Borland Room, a memorial to one of New England's best-loved nature writers, contains photos, a collection of the author's books, and even his manual Remington typewriter. Borland's first outdoor essay appeared in the *New York Times* in the fall of 1941. In the ensuing years, he wrote some 1,200 more. A selection of these essays was published in 1964 under the title *Sundial of the Seasons*. Borland's other books about nature include *An American Year*; *This Hill, This Valley*; *The Enduring Pattern*; and *Beyond Your Doorstep.*

Although Borland was born in Nebraska and spent much of his boyhood on a homestead in eastern Colorado, during much of his adult life he lived with his wife, Barbara, in a country house in Salisbury, Connecticut, on the Housatonic River. From his observations of this hill and valley country in northwestern Connecticut, he drew the inspiration for his books and essays about the natural world.

The Sharon Audubon Center has a Hal Borland Trail, 0.75 mile long, which begins near the native wildflower garden and continues through brushland and deciduous forest to a streamside hemlock forest.

What came to my mind on that warm, perfect May day of sunshine, spring flowers, and new growth everywhere was the chapter on woodlands in *Beyond Your Doorstep*. Borland writes that to find an abundance of spring wildflowers, one should seek out a patch of deciduous woodland on a slope facing southeast. Here the plants can grow in the deep leaf mold and receive the sunlight they need from mid-October until mid-May. Most of these early spring wildflowers blossom and then die back before summer's canopy of leaves shuts out the sunlight. About 55 species of wildflowers bloom in the area during March, April, and May. May is the time to look for the pink and yellow lady's slippers, blue wood violets, and jack-in-the-pulpits amid flowering dogwood.

A natural history interpretive area in the main building includes live exhibits of amphibians, reptiles, and raptors that are native to Connecticut. Visitors can see wood and box turtles in an exhibit on turtles of northwestern Connecticut. A pond life display includes spotted turtles. Due to loss of habitat, the population of these beautiful turtles is declining in New England.

The goal of the center's Wild Bird Rehabilitation Program is to treat and release all birds back into the wild. However, in some cases, nonreleasable raptors are retained for educational purposes, thus affording visitors an opportunity to learn about these species up close. This explains the presence of a pair of saw-whet owls along with a merlin that was brought to the Audubon Center in the fall of 1966. A collision with a golf ball during fall migration left the merlin with a shattered back shoulder, unable to sustain flight. The center is also now home to Princess, a perfectly healthy American crow. Unfortunately, Princess, who was raised by a loving family in West Cornwall, doesn't know that she is a crow. Not only does her trust in humans pose a threat to her safety, but she is unable to fit into crow "society."

In the gift shop and bookstore, I picked up a trail map and guide to the sanctuary grounds and 11 miles of trails. Near the main building is the native wildflower garden, where Virginia bluebells, columbine, and white violets were in bloom. The garden was planted and is maintained by the Sharon Garden Club.

I walked Fern Trail, a narrow, rocky woodland trail, one mile long, that follows the northern shore of Ford Pond. On this day in May, the pond reflected the sky and all the pastel shades of the spring foliage. A pair of Canada geese and their downy young swam near the shore. Near the dam and waterfall and the ice house that was part of the original farm, a colorful butterfly/hummingbird garden has been established. Blue and pink lupin, yellow iris, red clover, and white daisies were in bloom while blue forget-me-nots and purple iris flourished in wet areas by the stream and along the shore of the pond.

More than 70 species of birds may be seen on a spring bird walk on sanctuary grounds. Sightings in mid-May of 1998

included black-throated blue and black-throated green warblers, pine and palm warblers, and the Louisiana waterthrush
along with a scarlet tanager, yellow-bellied sapsucker, winter
wren, killdeer, and the northern oriole.

As I walked Fern Trail, I found many varieties of ferns,
including Christmas, maidenhair, New York, sensitive, wood
fern, and cinnamon ferns. Early in May, you'll also find blue
and yellow violets in bloom along this trail.

The Hendrickson Bog Meadow Trail is a loop walk of 1.6
miles through deciduous woodlands and along the edge of
Bog Meadow Pond, where you may see signs of beaver activity. You pass through a lovely high meadow with a few cedar,
white birch, and white pine trees. From there I walked
through a stand of pine to the shore of Bog Meadow Pond.
Surrounded by wetlands and hills on the farther shore, this
pond offers a feeling of remoteness. I sat under a huge maple
on the shore and watched for wildlife. Red-winged blackbirds
called from the marshes, and the surrounding woods were
filled with birdsong.

Other trails to explore are Ford Trail, 1.6 miles through
deciduous and hemlock forest; Hazelnut Trail, a short loop
trail one mile long; and Woodchuck Trail, 2.35 miles through
open fields and deciduous forest, which gives you a great
view to the west; and Lucy Harvey Trail, 0.3 mile long, "especially for the very young, the elderly, the disabled, and short-
walk enthusiasts." After a morning walk on the trails, you can
enjoy a picnic lunch at tables on the lawn near the main
building.

Part of the work of the center involves the Wild Bird
Rehabilitation Program. (Mammals and reptiles are referred
to other local wildlife rehabilitators.) As many as 150 birds
may be cared for during a given year. Birds that have been
cared for at the center include an American kestrel with a

broken wing and a red-tailed hawk suffering from a gunshot wound.

While it is sick or injured birds that are most often brought to the center, during the severe winter of 1993–94, the Sharon Audubon Center suddenly found itself playing host to horned grebes that had become stranded in northwestern Connecticut. Grebes are small diving and swimming water birds. In all, there are 26 species, 6 of which are found in North America. Those seen in Connecticut usually migrate from their summer range in northwestern Canada to the Atlantic Coast to spend the winter. Along the coast and in lakes and estuaries, they feed on small fish, shrimp and other crustaceans, and insects. That winter, because of the severe cold, grebes that strayed inland found all bodies of water frozen. Mistaking dark, wet roads and parking lots for open water, they landed on them in search of food. Needing an expanse of open water from which to take flight, these birds found themselves stranded. Over the course of the winter, a total of seven horned grebes were fortunate to be rescued by caring persons who took them to the Sharon Audubon Center. Here they were content to swim in the library bathtub and feed on minnows. Each consumed a dozen or more every day. After a checkup and their fill of fish, the grebes were driven to Grass Island in Greenwich, Connecticut, and released into Long Island Sound. Those who work in the wildlife rehabilitation program say that the most satisfying part of their work is being able to release a bird back into the wild.

Two separate buildings at the center house the educational facilities for the Northeast Region of the National Audubon Society. An educational program brings more than 5,000 school children to the Sharon Audubon Center each year. Summer environmental programs for different age groups are also offered, as well as a series of weekend environmental programs for adults and children. Spring programs include an Owl Prowl and Woodcock Walk in March, a Beaver Walk and a Wildlife Rehabilitation Workshop in April, and an Amphibian Walk in May.

Where: Two miles southeast of Sharon on State 4.

Hours: Grounds open daily, dawn to dusk, year-round. The center is open Monday to Saturday from 9:00 A.M. to 5:00 P.M. and Sunday from 1:00 P.M. to 5:00 P.M. (Closed on many holidays—call ahead.)

Admission: A small fee is charged for admission to the trails. No additional charge for attending most weekend environmental programs. Fees vary for the summer environmental programs for children. Those who join Friends of the Sharon Audubon Center receive free admission to the trails as well as other discounts.

Best time to visit: Spring to see wildflowers; spring and fall for migrating birds; otherwise, any season of the year is a good time.

Activities: Bird- and wildlife watching; wildflower walks; hiking; wildflower, herb and butterfly/hummingbird gardens; photography; picnicking; cross-country skiing; snowshoeing; and environmental programs for adults and children, including classes, workshops, walks, and special events.

Pets: The general policy is that no pets are allowed. However, in the spring of 1998, in response to requests from visitors, the policy was modified, on a trial basis, to allow dogs, on a leash, on selected trails. If you plan to bring your dog, check with the center first.

For more information: National Audubon Society, Sharon Audubon Center, 325 Cornwall Bridge Road, Sharon, CT 06069. Call 860-364-0520 (Monday to Friday from 9:00 A.M. to 5:00 P.M.).

Macedonia Brook State Park

Located in Kent, in mountainous terrain near the New York State border, Macedonia Brook is one of Connecticut's largest state parks, notable for its unspoiled natural beauty, miles of hiking trails, abundant woodland bird species, and large natural campsites. Macedonia Brook with its deep gorge and waterfalls crosses the park. Some of the most appealing campsites are along the brook. Especially during spring and fall bird migrations, this is one of the best places in the state to camp and enjoy early-morning bird walks.

Established in 1918 with a gift of 1,552 acres from the White Memorial Foundation, the park now encompasses 2,300 acres and two mountain peaks, including Cobble Mountain, the highest point at 1,380 feet. The Connecticut Blue Trail crosses Cobble Mountain and several other peaks, from which you get fine views of the Catskill and Taconic Mountains in New York. Numerous streams add to the pleasure of hiking in this park. For a spectacular view of the gorge of Macedonia Brook, stop near the park entrance, where the remains of a forge operated by the Kent Iron Company in the mid-1800s is located. The forge was a stamping works that required vast amounts of charcoal, which led to the destruction of the original forests by 1848.

Visiting the park today, you detect little hint of the region's early history as a center of industry. In fact, the huge maples along the park road seem always to have been part of the landscape. I first visited this park some years ago on a beautiful October day. With the abundance of maple trees, the woods were a symphony of color. After eating lunch at a sunny picnic table, I hiked the park road that follows Macedonia Brook, enjoying the bright foliage, the crisp crunch of dry leaves underfoot, and the sound of the swiftly flowing brook.

A trail map is available from the park office. You can climb the trail to the summit of Cobble Mountain or follow any one of a number of less strenuous loop trails. Most of the trails start from the park road. In general, those to the east of the road are less steep than the trails to the west.

Also available from the park office is a map of the portion of the Appalachian Trail (AT) that passes through northwestern Connecticut. Part of the trail has been relocated so that it no longer passes through Macedonia Brook State Park. However, you can gain access to the AT from State 341, just south of the park. The old segment of the AT that passes through the park is now part of the Blue Trail system.

This is one park that doesn't seem to be overcrowded, not even on summer weekends. On a clear, warm Sunday in late August, I found plenty of campsites available and uncrowded trails for hiking. The 84 spacious sites are grouped in four separate campgrounds. In addition to the sites along Macedonia Brook in Hickory Campground, you can choose from sites in Birch Campground or the more distant Overlook and Maple Campgrounds. My favorite site is tucked away in Upper Birch Campground on a hillside beneath a huge white pine. Facilities include fireplaces, water from an old-fashioned pump, and outhouses. It's a good idea to bring an insect repellent, because blackflies linger in these forests even as late as August.

Like the campsites, the picnic sites are spread out over a spacious area. A large stone and wood picnic pavilion can be used by groups or for shelter on rainy days. Some camp and picnic sites, including the pavilion, are accessible to people with disabilities.

The ranger on duty that August day reported seeing quail, white-tailed deer, and raccoons in the park. Ruffed grouse are common, and many hawks had also been observed that morning. Later, from a picnic site, I watched a red-tailed hawk soaring over the park and heard its high-pitched scream. This large, common hawk with a wingspan of 48 inches has a whitish breast and rust-colored tail. It prefers deciduous forests with adjacent open country and feeds mainly on small rodents.

This is also a fine area to see woodland bird species, especially during the spring and fall migrations. In May, the trees may be filled with warblers moving through the park. Species that nest in the area include black-and-white, blue-winged, black-throated blue, and golden-winged warblers. Other songbirds that nest in these woods are thrushes, winter wrens, scarlet tanagers, and rose-breasted grosbeaks.

In spring, anglers come to this park to enjoy stream fishing. Macedonia Brook is annually stocked with trout. Along with the opportunity to see birds, spring camping provides the possibility of having pan-fried brook trout for breakfast!

In winter, this is a good park for cross-country skiing. This area of northwestern Connecticut often has snow cover even when the ground is bare elsewhere in the state. Check with the park office before you go for information on which trails are suitable for skiing.

Where: Four miles north of Kent off State 341.
Hours: Open daily for day use from 8:00 A.M. to sunset, year-round, as conditions permit. Campgrounds open from the third weekend in April through the last weekend in September. Check with the park office first if you are planning to camp before Memorial Day or after Labor Day.
Admission: No charge for day use. A daily fee is charged for camping.
Best time to visit: During spring and fall migrations to see record numbers of birds. Otherwise, any season is a good time to enjoy this park.

Activities: Hiking, bird-watching, camping, stream fishing, picnicking, horseback riding, and cross-country skiing. Camping, picnicking, and horseback riding are accessible to those with disabilities. No ranger-led activities, but rangers are available during the summer season to answer questions. Trail maps are available at the park office.

Concessions: None.

Pets: Pets are not allowed in campgrounds or near streams.

For more information: Macedonia Brook State Park, 159 Macedonia Brook Road, Kent, CT 06757. Call campground office, 860-927-4100; park office, 860-927-3238.

Other: To promote a safer, more enjoyable camping experience, alcoholic beverages are prohibited in this campground.

Kent Falls State Park

Three miles north of Kent on U.S. 7 in the Litchfield Hills is one of my favorite state parks and one of Connecticut's most dramatic waterfalls. Kent Falls State Park, which covers 275 acres, was a gift to the state in 1919 by the White Memorial Foundation. The falls, formed by the waters of Falls Brook, drop 80 feet in the upper cascade, which must be reached by foot, while a series of lesser falls over steep rocky slopes and ledges of white marble bring the total drop to 200 feet. The falls are most spectacular in the spring, when the volume of water is greatest, but, for me, it is the sight of the lower falls framed by October's brilliant colors that comes to mind. Surrounded by the bright gold of the hickories, the crimson leaves of the maple trees, and the dark green of the hemlocks, the cascading water is an unforgettable sight that attracts photographers as well as those who enjoy hiking, fishing, or a picnic.

While there is no swimming in the park, wading in the pool at the base of the lower falls is a good way to cool off on a hot day. Children can explore for hours in and around the small pools of the brook, and stream fishermen can enjoy fly-casting for trout.

The picnic area is spread out through the park and has some choice tables with a view of the falls as well as some large secluded picnic sites that were at one time campsites.

I have visited this park many times and seldom drive by it without stopping, but one time that I especially remember is the early October day when two friends and I hiked the trail to the upper falls. What started out as an impromptu picnic turned into a real feast, for Angela, Mary, and I lingered a long time, enjoying the food, the warm sun, the fall foliage, and the splendid view of the falls.

It was midafternoon by the time we approached the rustic staired pathway, constructed by the Youth Conservation Corps, that leads to the upper falls. A forest of hemlocks clings to the steep hillside and shelters a garden of ferns and mosses. Looking down, we had a fine view of the gorge carved through the rock walls by the force of water. We found potholes where the swirling water had worn away the softer layers of rock. Here and there, a side trail leads to the rocky gorge, where you'll find sunlit pools of water and close-up views of the cascading waters of the upper falls. We were enveloped in the cool and quiet of the forest, where the only sounds were those of falling water and the call of a chickadee. Climbing higher, we reached the top of the falls, where the water, surrounded by a halo of golden leaves, caught the sunlight. The view from here is well worth the climb. Often when the cold rains of November or the ice storms of January or February keep me inside, I recall that sunny, golden day spent in the hills of northwestern Connecticut.

Kent Falls at Kent Falls State Park

Spring, summer, and fall are all good times to visit. While it may be crowded on a summer weekend, the ample parking and well-spaced picnic sites provide room for one more person or family to enjoy this park.

Where: Three miles north of Kent on U.S. 7.
Hours: Daily, from 8:00 A.M. to sunset.
Admission: Entrance fee on weekends and holidays from April 17 through October 25.
Best time to visit: Spring or fall for viewing the falls or hik-

ing. Spring for fishing. Any season to enjoy a picnic. Bring insect repellent, as blackflies may be present even in late summer.

Activities: Picnicking, fishing, hiking, and photography. No ranger-led activities are offered.

Concessions: None. However, you may often find an ice-cream vendor in the parking area on summer weekends.

Pets: Permitted on a leash in the picnic area. Not allowed near the falls or brook.

Amenities: Free parking, picnic tables, rest rooms, and drinking water. Facilities accessible to disabled people include the parking area, picnic tables, and a telephone.

For more information: State Parks Division, Bureau of Outdoor Recreation, Connecticut Department of Environmental Protection, 79 Elm Street, Hartford, CT 06106-5127. Call 860-424-3200. Website: www.dep.state.ct.us.

Lake Waramaug State Park

Surely, Lake Waramaug, surrounded by forests and the Litchfield Hills, is one of Connecticut's most prized lakes. Located in Kent and New Preston, it has been compared to Switzerland's Lake Lucerne, and few bodies of water in the state can rival its splendor when the bright hues of autumn are reflected in its blue depths. At the head of the lake, Lake Waramaug State Park occupies 95 acres along the west shore. It's one of my favorite destinations for camping, swimming, picnicking, and canoeing.

Lake Waramaug was named for the chief of the Wyantenock Indians, who once used the area as their hunting grounds. The park is part of some 4,000 acres of land within the geographical boundaries of the town of Kent that have been set aside as parks or public lands. Macedonia Brook and

Kent Falls are the other state parks. Together they preserve some of Connecticut's finest natural areas.

Kent's early settlers, however, viewed the wilderness as an enemy to be conquered. The town became the center of an early iron-making industry. On the grounds of the Sloane-Stanley Museum are the remains of an old iron-smelting furnace of the Kent Iron Company, which was in operation from 1826 to 1896. The furnaces used charcoal as fuel, and thousands of trees were cut for the charcoal kilns. Others were taken for lumber to build houses, leaving the hills bare and ugly. The iron industry has been gone for almost a hundred years, time enough for a fine second-growth forest to make the hills lush and green again.

In summer, Lake Waramaug State Park is a prime destination for swimming and a picnic, or perhaps an afternoon of canoeing along the park's undeveloped west shore. From Memorial Day through Labor Day weekend, North American Canoe Tours rents canoes and pedal boats. The clear water and sand beach make for enjoyable swimming and shaded picnic tables overlooking the lake provide a cool place to eat lunch.

Lake Waramaug State Park also has one of Connecticut's most attractive campgrounds, with 88 well-spaced sites in a grassy, shaded area overlooking the lake. Services include a food concession and modern rest rooms with showers. You may camp here from May 15 to September 30.

In 1997, a $1.3 million plan was approved for improving facilities, including repaving the roadways and construction of a new entrance booth, rest rooms, and a new maintenance center. There is also a proposal to construct a public boat launch on Lake Waramaug, most likely at the state park. This has raised some fears about the environmental impact of increased use and the concern that boats from the outside will bring in Eurasian milfoil, a plant that is choking other lakes in Connecticut.

For spectacular scenery, most would agree that the best time to visit this park is mid-October, when the trees lining the lake shore turn to brilliant shades of red and gold. I remember one bright October day when my friend Katherine and I followed the narrow, winding shore road, nine miles in length, that encircles the lake. It is best to do this on a weekday when traffic is light and you can give your undivided attention to the views of water and foliage that unfold at every turn in the road.

In winter, the lake's frozen surface becomes a great place for an afternoon of ice skating. You may want to combine a winter outing with a fireside dinner or Sunday brunch at the Lakeview Inn (formerly the Inn on Lake Waramaug), located near the state park at 107 North Shore Road in New Preston. It is one of the area's charming country inns that attract visitors year-round.

Where: Five miles north of New Preston off State 45 on Lake Waramaug Road.

Hours: Open daily for day use from 8:00 A.M. to sunset. The campground is open from May 15 to September 30. Campsites are available for rental until 10:00 P.M. each evening.

Admission: There is a day-use fee weekends and holidays from Memorial Day through Labor Day weekend. Campers pay a nightly fee per campsite.

Best time to visit: Weekdays in summer for swimming, canoeing, and camping. Advance reservations for campsites are advisable during the summer season. Try spring or fall for uncrowded camping. Mid-October is usually the best time for fall foliage viewing.

Activities: A Camper Nature Program is offered in the summer, with rangers on duty during the camping season. Swimming, picnicking, camping, canoeing, fishing, scuba diving, hiking, and ice skating. Facilities for camping and picnick-

ing, including a picnic shelter, are accessible to visitors with disabilities.
Concessions: A food concession is
open during the summer season.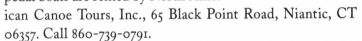
Also during the summer, canoes and
pedal boats are rented by North Amer-
ican Canoe Tours, Inc., 65 Black Point Road, Niantic, CT
06357. Call 860-739-0791.
Pets: Not permitted.
For more information: Lake Waramaug State Park, 30 Lake
Waramaug Road, New Preston, CT 06777. Call campground
office: 860-868-0220; park office: 860-868-2592.

Applications for campsite reservations must be received at
least 10 days in advance. They are accepted by mail beginning January 15, and they should be sent directly to the
campground.

Lakeview Inn, 107 North Shore Road, New Preston, CT
06777. Open for lunch and dinner, closed Tuesday. Call 860-
868-1000.

Mount Tom State Park

On a bright, windy, cool day that was more like October than
early September, I drove to Mount Tom State Park, located off
U.S. 202, west of the center of Litchfield. This 233-acre park
is memorable for its fine sand beach, excellent swimming,
waterfront picnic sites, and the Tower Trail, which affords a
marvelous view from the crest of Mount Tom.

The park has tables and fireplaces, bathhouses, rest rooms,
and a food concession. Drinking water is available from a
hand pump.

The major portion of the park was donated by Charles H.
Sneff and his wife, Gustavia, in 1911. It is believed to be the

first gift to the state of land valued mainly for its great natural beauty.

The 62-acre pond found in the park is largely spring-fed with clear, deep water. Development is limited to some private cottages on the opposite shore. Because no motors are permitted on the pond, it is a good place for canoes. You can also launch a car-top fishing boat or small sailboat. The pond is stocked with trout.

On hot summer days, the beach area may be crowded, but with many other picnic tables scattered in wooded areas of the park, you can usually find a quiet spot for yourself even on summer weekends.

An off-season visit has its own advantages. On that September day, while eating lunch and drinking a welcome cup of hot coffee, I watched two brave girls go swimming! They declared the water to be "nice and invigorating." Another bonus, they had the sand beach and swimming area all to themselves. In the off-season, also, the marshy area on the opposite shore of the pond is a good place to observe waterfowl. I saw black ducks and mallards that day.

Behind the waterfront area, on the wooded hillside, you will find the beginning of the 1.5-mile Tower Trail, which follows a moderately steep gravel road. In spring, the white blossoms of shadbush light up the woods. As you hike, look for the characteristic rectangular holes drilled by pileated woodpeckers. They are usually found on dying trees that have been invaded by colonies of black carpenter ants. Especially in winter, these birds may actually help save the life of a tree by feeding on the ants until the colony is destroyed, enabling the tree to recover. If you're lucky, you may catch a glimpse of this spectacular crow-sized woodpecker, with its bright red crest, or hear the sound of its drilling echoing through the woods. This bird usually builds its nest in the tall stub of a dead tree, in dense forest, well hidden by the surrounding leafy branches of live trees.

The trail ends at the summit of Mount Tom (at an elevation of 1,325 feet), near a stone tower that is 34 feet high. From the roof of the tower, a marvelous view of Mount Tom Pond is spread out before you far below. To the northwest is the Riga Plateau, and to the right are Bantam Lake and the white church spires of Litchfield. If the day is really clear, you can even see Long Island Sound to the south.

The round-trip hike takes only about an hour, but, of course, you will want time to spend on the summit enjoying the view; and combining the hike with swimming or canoeing and a picnic makes for an ideal day in the outdoors.

Where: Seven and a half miles west of Litchfield off U.S. 202. Look for the "State Park" sign on the left after passing a view of Mount Tom Pond.

Hours: Daily, from 8:00 A.M. to sunset, year-round, as conditions permit.

Admission: Parking fee Memorial Day through Labor Day weekend.

Best time to visit: Spring and fall for hiking and boating. Summer for swimming. Bring insect repellent to discourage blackflies in spring and early summer.

Activities: Swimming, scuba diving, picnicking, fishing, canoeing, sailing, hiking, fall foliage viewing, ice skating.

Concessions: A food concession featuring fare such as hamburgers and hot dogs, chili, ice cream, soft drinks, and coffee, is in operation during the summer months and weekends in the fall.

Pets: Not allowed on the beach. Pets on a leash are permitted on the Tower Trail.

Other: Camping is available nearby at the White Memorial Foundation's two campgrounds and at two private campgrounds: Hemlock Hill Camp Resort, P.O. Box 828, Hemlock

Hill Road, Litchfield, CT 06759. Call 860-567-2267. Looking Glass Hill Campground, P.O. Box 1610, Litchfield, CT 06759. Call 860-567-2050.

For more information: State Parks Division, Bureau of Outdoor Recreation, Connecticut Department of Environmental Protection, 79 Elm Street, Hartford, CT 06106-5127. Call 860-424-3200. Website: www.dep.state.ct.us.

White Memorial Foundation and Conservation Center

The largest wildlife refuge in Connecticut, the White Memorial Foundation consists of some 4,000 acres of woodland, open fields, ponds, marshland, and Bantam Lake shore property in the towns of Litchfield and Morris. This natural treasure owes its existence to the foresight and generosity of two local residents, Alain C. White and his sister, May W. White. Feeling that the lake and surrounding countryside should be preserved for the public to enjoy, the Whites, between 1908 and 1912, purchased several large tracts of land, extending north and east of Bantam Lake. In 1913, they conveyed the land as the White Memorial Foundation, Inc. In addition to the gift of land, the Whites added an endowment to help with the cost of development and maintenance of the property. The White Memorial Conservation Center houses a Nature Museum and one of the finest nature libraries in the state.

A wide range of facilities for outdoor study and recreation includes 35 miles of beautifully maintained trails, campgrounds, boating facilities, meetinghouses, and special areas for large indoor gatherings.

Nature Museum

A two-year, $1 million museum renovation project, designed by Harrison (Whitey) Jenkins of West Hartford, was completed in the spring of 1998. Entitled, "A Journey Through White Memorial," the museum's goal is telling the story of the White Memorial property from approximately 12,000 years ago to the present day.

Entering the museum, you notice cloud formations overhead and listen to sounds of nature as you are transported back to a time when glaciers covered the hills and valleys of Litchfield County. Most of New England's lakes and ponds were created by glaciers, including Bantam Lake.

You learn about the first inhabitants, the Pootatuck Indian Tribe. While Native Americans made careful use of natural resources and "lived close to the land without overtaking it," Europeans exploited the land, making changes that destroyed the forests and led to a decline in forest wildlife. It was not until the mid- to late-1900s, after much of the agricultural land had been abandoned, that forest growth began to return and with it some species of wildlife such as the bobcat, black bear, and wild turkey.

The museum exhibits transport you back into each historical period and provide a clear picture of life at that time. There's an exhibit on the history of the White family, who moved to Litchfield in 1863. Explore White Memorial's Habitat Diversity and learn a great deal about the five different habitat types, the plant and animal species that each supports, and how all are important in the web of life.

Through photographic murals, wonderful dioramas showing native wildlife, and hands-on exhibits, you can visit Little Pond and the boardwalk, watch beaver at the river's edge, and visit Pine Island in spring and observe its wildlife, including a mink, flying squirrel, and red-winged blackbirds. A return to Pine Island in winter reveals a saw-whet owl and pine grosbeaks as well as life below the surface of the land, where, in the comparative warmth of insulating mud, turtles, snakes, and salamanders hibernate and wait for spring.

There's a wonderful diorama, a fall foliage scene, depicting a white-tailed deer at the edge of Bantam Lake, as well as one in the main entry where you are greeted by a yearling black bear.

In the section of the museum on Upland Hardwoods, you visit Beaver Pond in the early morning and observe a gray fox that has caught a red squirrel, while a summer walk in Catlin Woods reveals a rich variety of wildlife, including ruffed grouse, great horned owl, northern goshawk, pileated woodpecker, red squirrel, and a raccoon.

Afternoon at the Plunge Pool depicts a bobcat that has just had a successful hunt and a gray squirrel attempting to escape from a broad-winged hawk.

Interactive stations, including identifying backyard wildlife, make learning fun for adults and children. Then, take time to visit the observation area where you can sit and watch the wild birds outside as they visit the bird-feeder sculpture garden.

Leaving the museum, you are invited to "Explore, Discover, Respect" as you walk the trails. Both the museum and the preserve are places that you will wish to return to often.

The Mattatuck Dark Sky Observatory

On May 10, 1997, the Mattatuck Astronomical Society held an official opening and dedication ceremony at this new observatory located on top of a hill known as Sawmill Field. The 12-by-14-foot roll-off roof structure houses a 17½-inch Newtonian-reflecting telescope and is ideally situated for both amateur astronomical research and public viewing of the night sky. Public observing sessions are listed in *Sanctuary*, the newsletter of the White Memorial Conservation Center.

Nature Trail

Before attempting to explore any of the trails, visit the bookstore and its gift shop and purchase one of the excellent trail maps.

On a bright, warm day in mid-September, I hiked the self-guiding Nature Trail that begins near the museum. It is an easy trail to hike, about one-half mile long, with 17 marked stations, which are interpreted in a guide you can purchase for a small fee in the museum store.

The start of the trail is lined with tall sugar maples. To the right is an open field that is used for activities, but it is also home to birds and animals that live in open spaces. Looking closely, you may see a woodchuck, cottontail rabbit, or wild turkey. A spreading oak tree often produces a large crop of acorns, providing food for the squirrels, wild turkeys, wood ducks, and blue jays that inhabit the refuge. The trail passes through a white-pine forest and then turns left toward the Bantam River.

From the forest, I emerged into a marsh area where grasses, sedges, and shrubs provide food and shelter for many species of wildlife. Ducks, great blue herons, rails, marsh wrens, swamp sparrows, and red-winged blackbirds are often seen here and in other open marsh areas. To the right of the marsh, near the river, I found the shrubs filled with songbirds— chickadees, white-breasted nuthatches, eastern phoebes, and several species of warblers that I found hard to identify as they flew from branch to branch or were concealed by the dense shrubbery.

The portion of the trail that follows the Bantam River is a special delight. Here I watched a flock of black ducks. On another day, I watched a canoeist paddle the slow-moving river, which meanders through the northern half of the White Memorial Foundation. A canoe trip is an ideal way to look for waterfowl and wading birds that frequent the river and surrounding wetlands. River otters are occasionally seen. If you own a canoe, by all means bring it with you.

From the river the trail turns left, and I found myself in an old-growth forest. A large pine, well over 200 years old and three feet in diameter, towered 100 feet above the forest floor. Most of the smaller trees are eastern hemlock, which are very tolerant of shade. As I walked, I noticed depressions and mounds on the forest floor. These signify that it is an old forest. Many of the low areas were created when trees, now long gone, became uprooted, leaving hollows in the earth. The mounds were formed by the long-since-decayed root masses of the big trees.

Looking down, I noticed the evergreen plants growing on the forest floor: goldthread, shining club moss, and partridge berries. In the soft, wet mud of a low area, I found deer tracks. Beneath a tree, I discovered a number of owl pellets. If you can locate an owl's feeding roost, you have a good chance of seeing the bird if you return to the woods after dark.

Holbrook Bird Observatory

Back at the parking area, I picked up my lunch and headed for one of the picnic tables near the Holbrook Bird Observatory. The observatory, which has 30 sheltered viewing stations available for bird-watchers and photographers, overlooks an area landscaped with shrubs that attract a variety of birds in all seasons. A bird-feeding station is filled with food during the winter months. With the aid of a pair of binoculars, you can combine eating lunch with bird-watching.

Butterfly Habitats

Located off the Ongley Pond Trail, just south of the museum, is a Butterfly Garden, which was designed and planted by the Litchfield Garden Club in 1998. Located on a slope between a field and the pond (both important habitat requirements for butterflies), the garden attracts not only butterflies but honeybees, hummingbirds, and other nectar lovers as well. A stone bench installed by the garden club invites visitors to sit and enjoy the garden and its wildlife.

A second butterfly and wildflower garden, located next to the Museum's Outdoor Bird Sanctuary exhibit, was renovated during the summer of 1998 by Paul Sakren, an active volunteer and authority on medicinal plants. Sakren has not only expanded the garden, but has increased the diversity of the plants as well.

Lake Trail

During the afternoon, I hiked the Lake Trail, which is one mile in length and leads to a bird-observation platform overlooking Bantam Lake. I walked past fields of goldenrod and purple asters before entering the North Bay Natural Area, which includes the wetland habitats at the north end of Bantam Lake's North Bay. The most common trees in the swamp are red maples. This swamp is home to water thrushes, grouse, vireos, yellowthroats, woodpeckers, and nuthatches.

Nearer the shore of the lake, where the soil is dry for at least part of the summer, is an area of high willows. To the north is a ridge composed of lake-bottom mud and rocks, fashioned over the years by the winter forces of nature, which cause the water to freeze, then expand and contract, producing great pressure on the bottom of the lake. The vegetation on this ridge is quite different from that in the surrounding swamp. In addition to red maple, I saw ash, elm, black willow, and red oak. At the edge of the lake is a thick growth of buttonbush, which flourishes in the shallow water.

Emerging from the swamp to the bird-observation platform was one of my most memorable moments while exploring White Memorial Foundation trails. From the platform, I had a marvelous view of North Bay and the marsh areas along the shore. Since it was mid-September and not a weekend, there was little human activity, and I felt as if I had reached the shore of a wilderness lake. Such an impression is rare, because during the summer there is considerable activity on Bantam Lake, the largest natural lake in Connecticut. Nevertheless, on this bright, clear afternoon, only one or two motorboats broke the stillness as I watched a flock of black ducks feeding in the marshes and several herring gulls flying overhead. Then I was surprised to see a double-crested cormorant—a rare sight in these inland waters—land on a concrete pier. The unique bird-observation platform was built in 1972 on the concrete piers of an old railroad that extended into the lake and was used when ice was harvested and shipped to New York City.

On the return hike, I came across some closed gentians growing with the goldenrod beside the trail. It has been years since I have seen those plants with their deep violet blue blossoms growing in the wild. They are among the loveliest wildflowers we have in Connecticut.

Some 165 different species of wildflowers grow on White Memorial Foundation lands. May is probably the most exciting month to see wildflowers. Fifty-six different species bloom during this month, including such beauties as white and painted trillium and the lovely pink lady's slipper known as moccasin flower.

Mattatuck Trail

Part of the Mattatuck Trail, one of Connecticut's best hiking trails, passes through White Memorial Foundation lands. The 35-mile-long trail starts at Mad River Road in Wolcott and crosses Prospect and Mohawk Mountains before joining the Appalachian Trail in Cornwall. If you hike the 6.2-mile segment of the trail that passes through the refuge, you will have an introduction to all the refuge's varied habitats except the shore of Bantam Lake. Species of wildlife that you may see include water thrushes and ducks at Beaver Pond; duck broods and swallows at Fawn Pond; and beaver, along with flycatchers and warblers, at Heron Pond. (The Heron Pond Trail, which is 0.6 mile in length, circles the pond and connects with the Mattatuck Trail.) The Mattatuck Trail then passes near Cranberry Pond, a good place to look for herons. Both the great blue and the green-backed heron nest in the refuge.

After passing through Catlin Woods, the trail crosses the Bantam River and intersects with Pine Island Trail near Duck Pond. As its name implies, Duck Pond is another good area to look for nesting ducks in the spring. Those nesting in the refuge include mallards, American black ducks, blue-winged teal, wood ducks, and hooded mergansers.

Little Pond Trail

Accessible from South Lake Street, Little Pond Trail includes a boardwalk that provides access to a wetland area frequented by herons, swallows, and ducks. In 1985, Hurricane Gloria caused significant damage to the original boardwalk. After nine years of labor by a White Memorial crew, a new board-walk was completed in August 1994. Little Pond is a special place, one of serene beauty, remote from the ugly scars of man's mechanized world. Walk the boardwalk in mid-June, when the wild yellow and blue iris are in bloom, and you will agree that it is indeed a magical place.

Camping

You will have an even better opportunity to see birds and other wildlife if you camp at one of the foundation's family campgrounds.

Point Folly has 47 sites on a peninsula that extends into Bantam Lake. The waterfront campsites are the kind you dream about on winter evenings. Tenting and trailer RV camping are allowed. The size of the trailer permitted depends on the site involved and is subject to the approval of the camp manager. Drinking water, pit toilets, and a dumping station are provided. Not provided are hookups for recreational vehicles, showers, or a shelter. A campground store and marina are located near the entrance to Point Folly. Public boat-launching facilities are available at the marina. Sandy Beach, located on Bantam Lake, can be used by campers for a nominal fee. The campground at Point Folly opens in early May and closes on Columbus Day.

The other campground, Windmill Hill, has 20 large sites shaded by pine, oak, and maple trees. Open from Memorial Day weekend through Labor Day, it is restricted to tent camping. In late September, when I walked through the campground, the only sounds I heard were the chatter of a pair of red squirrels and chickadees calling from the branches of the pine trees. In late fall, Windmill Hill is a good place to look for winter birds, including kinglets and, occasionally, pine grosbeaks.

Reservations for campsites are advisable and are accepted by mail only until Memorial Day weekend. After that, make your reservation in person at the campground store. Telephone reservations are not accepted. The minimum reservation is two days and three days on holiday weekends. The maximum stay is 14 days. All sites not reserved in advance are available on a first-come, first-served basis.

Both of these campgrounds are designed to offer a quiet, unspoiled camping experience and access to the wonders of nature to be found in the refuge.

I can't imagine a better inland area for birding in Connecticut than the White Memorial Foundation. As of spring of 1998, 249 species had been reported on foundation lands. Information in the foundation's *Guide to Birding* includes the times of the year species are seen, an indication of their abundance, and a record of those that nest in the refuge. Just to give you an idea of the wealth of bird life in the refuge, the list of breeding birds includes the ruby-throated hummingbird, pileated woodpecker, red-bellied woodpecker, great crested flycatcher, winter wren, eastern bluebird, blue-gray gnatcatcher, golden-crowned kinglet, many species of warblers, northern oriole, scarlet tanager, rose-breasted grosbeak, and the rare indigo bunting.

Camping at the White Memorial Foundation also provides the best opportunity to catch a glimpse of some of the mammals that make their home within the refuge, especially since many of these are active mainly at night. Commonly seen are red and gray squirrels, chipmunks, woodchucks, white-tailed deer, eastern coyotes, raccoons, and eastern cottontails. Seven species of bats have been seen in the refuge, with the little brown bat being the most common.

The less-often-seen species include mink, which prefer forested, log-strewn areas near streams and marshes. Muskrat are occasionally seen from the boardwalk around Little Pond.

Weasels and even the rare fisher, which prefers dense hard-wood-softwood forests, have been seen. The foundation's wet-lands are also home to the river otter, a playful animal that enjoys sliding down steep banks. Even the bobcat, which is making a comeback in Connecticut, has been spotted by museum staff, and sightings of black bear are becoming more frequent. As Jeff Greenwood, the center's director of educa-tion, pointed out, both the vast size of the preserve and the varied habitats contribute to the fact that unusual sightings of wildlife are more apt to occur here than elsewhere in Connecticut.

Cross-Country Skiing

In the winter, when there is snow, about 35 miles of trails are open for cross-country skiing and snowshoeing. Snowmobiles and all-terrain vehicles are not allowed. The trails, which are not groomed, are open to the public seven days a week. Most of the trails are relatively flat, but several are challenging, an attraction for more experienced skiers. No trail fee is charged. Trail maps may be purchased at the museum store. The activ-ity shed, located behind the museum, is open to skiers and is equipped with picnic tables and a woodstove. Outhouses are the only rest rooms provided.

Periodically during the winter, interpretive nature walks on skis are held on weekends. These are free to the public. Brief reports of snow depth and conditions may be obtained by call-ing the museum at 860-567-0857.

Where: The entrance to the White Memorial Foundation and Conservation Center is located about two miles west of Litch-field, off U.S. 202 on Whitehall Road.
Hours: The grounds are open daily 24 hours. The Conserva-tion Center, which houses the Nature Museum, gift shop, and

bookstore, is open Monday through Saturday from 9:00 A.M. to 5:00 P.M., Sunday from 12:00 P.M. to 5:00 P.M., April through October 26. For the rest of the year, the center is open Monday through Saturday from 8:30 A.M. to 4:30 P.M., Sunday from 12:00 P.M. to 4:00 P.M. Closed January 1, Easter Sunday, July 4, Thanksgiving (including the Friday after Thanksgiving), and December 25. The foundation office is open Monday through Friday 7:30 A.M. to 4:30 P.M.

Admission: No charge for use of the trails and roads for hiking, nature study, horseback riding on designated roads, or cross-country skiing. Weekend walks and most programs are also free of charge. However, many families and individuals choose to become members of the White Memorial Foundation in order to help support the foundation's goals in education, conservation, research, and recreation. Those who are not members pay a fee for admission to the museum; children under six years old are free. Campers pay a nightly camping fee. There is also a charge for having visitors at your campsite.

Best time to visit: Each season is special: spring for nesting birds and wildflowers, summer for camping and canoeing, autumn for fall bird migrations and the splendor of fall foliage in the Litchfield Hills, winter for cross-country skiing and looking for animal tracks and winter birds. Spring, summer, and fall are good for hiking, nature study, and horseback riding.

Activities: Hiking, picnicking, horseback riding, camping, canoeing, fishing for northern pike and bass, cross-country skiing, bicycling, bird-watching, orienteering, butterfly gardens, and weekend nature walks and other programs, including dark sky observing sessions.

Horses are allowed on designated woods roads and other roads throughout the refuge as shown on the White Memorial Guide Map. Horse-trailer parking is allowed along the edges of the Activity Field and Sawmill Field.

There is no place to rent a canoe in the immediate area, but Main Stream Canoes in New Hartford (860-379-6657) offers rentals as well as Collinsville Canoe & Kayak in Collinsville (860-693-6977), which also offers occasional canoe or kayak tours at White Memorial.

Rentals of cross-country ski equipment and snowshoes are available from the Wilderness Shop in Litchfield (860-567-5905).

Concessions: None.

Pets: Pets on a leash are allowed. If you are camping with your dog, it must be confined on a leash not more than seven feet in length, and you must stay with your pet at all times.

Other: Several publications, including the trail map, checklists for birds and wildflowers, and a guide to the Nature Trail, are available at the museum store. A section of the foundation property has been mapped for the increasingly popular sport of orienteering. There is also a complete range of facilities for group use, including the Carriage House with dormitories; dining and meeting facilities; and the Mott–Van Winkle Classroom, which is fully equipped and available for year-round group programs, with seating for 75 people, blackboards, and audiovisual facilities.

For more information: White Memorial Foundation and Conservation Center, P.O. Box 368, 71 Whitehall Road, Litchfield, CT 06759-0368. Call 860-567-0857.

Topsmead State Forest

Hidden away off Buell Road in Litchfield is a very special place—Topsmead State Forest. Topsmead is the former summer home of Edith M. Chase of Waterbury, daughter of Henry S. Chase, the first president of the Chase Brass Company of Waterbury. Designed by famed architect Richard

Henry Dana Jr., the Tudor-style "cottage" was completed in 1924. It is situated atop a 1,230-foot-high knoll from which you have a wonderful view out over the surrounding countryside to the distant hills. Flower gardens, rolling lawns, well-kept pastures, hayfields bordered by beautiful stone walls, and forestland are all part of the property. During her lifetime, Miss Chase, who was a former director of the Connecticut Forest and Park Association, was fond of roaming the fields and woods of her summer home. She liked to observe the many species of birds and wildflowers she found there. From the natural world, she drew a sense of renewal that enabled her to face again the challenges of the business world.

When Edith Chase died in 1972, she left Topsmead, which includes the summer home and 514 acres of land, to the people of Connecticut. It was her desire that Topsmead be managed to protect its natural beauty, allowing passive and casual recreational pursuits such as hiking, picnicking, nature study, cross-country skiing, and snowshoeing.

In planning for the future of the area, the Department of Environmental Protection called for development of a 40-acre wildflower preserve and a nature trail, which were constructed during the summers of 1974 and 1975 by the Connecticut Conservation Corps and dedicated to Edith M. Chase.

A right turn off Buell Road leads to the entrance to the parking area. Nearby you can pick up a trail map. The Edith Chase Ecology Trail and wildflower preserve are just north of the parking area. Look for the trail sign to the right of the small pond. This area of wooded wetlands is also an excellent site for observing songbirds, especially along the pond outlet brook. The northeast corner of the preserve has a natural small marsh that attracts plants and birds found only in a wetland habitat. The preserve is home to more than 200 plant species, including abundant wildflowers and ferns.

While spring is the best time to get your fill of wildflowers in bloom and also to observe nesting songbirds, the trail is worth walking at other seasons of the year as well. In early September, I heard the familiar calls of chickadees, nuthatches, and phoebes. In the groves of tall hemlocks, sunlight barely filtered through the dark branches, but the stands of swamp maple were already displaying a reddish tinge. Various trees and shrubs that provide food for wildlife have been added to provide a more diverse habitat. I observed squirrels and chipmunks busy with the task of storing a winter's food supply, and I heard, from deep in the marsh, the musical "ker-r-r-r-ock" of a leopard frog.

A picnic table near the pond is a good place to stop for lunch. Blue and white asters and feathery goldenrod were in bloom that September day, and the sweet smell of freshly cut hay filled the late-summer air.

Interpretive plaques erected by the Boy Scouts along the nature trail contain much information that will add to your understanding of the relationships between organisms and their environment. One sign, entitled "The Pyramid of Life," explains that the foundation of life is soil, which along with sunlight and rain produces plant life. All animals, including man, depend on plants directly or indirectly for energy. It concludes, "Man should know that all life depends on the soil; as the soil goes, so goes all life."

In 1998, the Department of Environmental Protection constructed a new 8-by-20-foot wooden viewing blind at the edge of a field as part of a program begun in the mid-1990s to create special places in state parks and forests where people can have a chance to experience wildlife in its natural surroundings. From this blind, you may see bobolinks and the rare meadowlark, which has recently been added as a species of special concern to the state's endangered species list. Other birds you may see from the blind include kestrels, bluebirds, red-tailed hawks, and indigo buntings. Watching white-tailed deer or a coyote or fox out hunting is another possibility.

Back at the parking lot, I picked up my lunch and walked up the road to the Tudor-style cottage. Magnificent tall pines and hemlocks line the road. On this clear, warm afternoon, the view out over the surrounding countryside was impressive. Topsmead, built of masonry and cypress with a slate roof, contains most of its original furnishings. It is open to the public during the summer and fall on designated days. From here, you have your choice of several miles of hiking and cross-country ski trails, roads, and open fields that invite exploration.

Horseback riding is permitted on certain trails, and I followed one that led between high fields bordered by handsome stone walls. When you live in a wooded valley as I do, you really appreciate being in this wide-open country where you can see for miles. Monarchs and spangled fritillaries glided over the fields, stopping to feed on the goldenrod and asters that blossomed by the side of the road. On the way back, I caught my breath as an eastern bluebird flew across the field and perched on a branch in a large pine tree. This was an exciting moment because it had been many years since I had seen a bluebird in Connecticut. The population of this once-common bird declined due to the use of insecticides, competition from other birds such as starlings, and the disappearance of the old orchards that were its favorite nest sites. Not only is there an orchard at Topsmead, but nesting boxes have been erected in the fields to provide additional sites. Bluebirds feed on a varied diet that includes grasshoppers, beetles, flying insects, and caterpillars, as well as berries and other fruit.

You'll find picnic tables placed at inviting sites, but you are also encouraged to spread your blanket out and enjoy your lunch wherever you choose. Picnic fires are not permitted. One family had come by bicycle and was having a picnic in the shade of a huge maple. A group of horseback riders passed along the trail. An artist was setting up his easel, and a young woman had come in search of a quiet place to read.

While hiking at Topsmead, you may see white-tailed deer. Look for them feeding in the fields at the edge of the woods early in the morning or toward dusk. The orchard, when there are apples on the ground, is another likely spot. In the winter, you can sometimes follow deer tracks on skis or snowshoes. During severe winter storms, they often gather in dense stands of evergreens, especially hemlocks, which are a favorite winter food. After a fresh snowstorm, you can find their bedding spots in these sheltered areas.

In the high fields or near the brushy edges of woods, you may see woodchucks. They are daytime animals. Clover and alfalfa are favorite foods, but they eat a variety of plants, not to mention cultivated vegetables if they can find such gourmet fare. A shrill whistle is their cry of alarm.

You will probably not see raccoons, which are active mainly at night. Should you see one, a park sign warns visitors not to approach this animal because of its susceptibility to rabies, which has now spread from the mid-Atlantic region into most areas of Connecticut.

One of the plaques along the nature trail gives the following prescription for survival: "Man in balance with nature in a peaceful world." Walking the trails at Topsmead, one feels that here, at least, that vision has been achieved.

Where: From the intersection of State 63 and 118 in the center of Litchfield, drive two miles east on State 118. Turn right on East Litchfield Road. In one-half mile, turn right onto Buell Road.

Hours: The state forest is open daily from 8:00 A.M. until dusk, year-round, as conditions permit. The Topsmead "cottage" is open weekends, noon to 5:00 P.M., June through October, on the second and fourth weekends of the month.

Admission: Free to the public.

Best time to visit: Anytime during the year: spring for wildflowers and nesting songbirds, autumn for fall foliage walks, and winter for cross-country skiing.

Activities: Hiking, bird-watching and nature study, picnicking, horseback riding, cross-country skiing, snowshoeing, and sledding. Tours of the Chase summer home.

Concessions: None.

Pets: Permitted on a leash.

Other: Trail maps are available at an information station near the parking area. However, except when the house is open to the public, there is generally no ranger on duty to answer questions about the trails or wildlife.

For more information: Topsmead State Forest, Buell Road, Litchfield, CT 06759. Call 860-567-5694.

Flanders Nature Center

Flanders Nature Center in Woodbury is a wonderful place to observe wildlife or simply to enjoy an afternoon hike on well-marked and maintained trails. A drive of about 10 miles north from I-84 in Southbury transports you into another world, where land is managed for the benefit of wildlife as well as man and where traffic and shopping malls seem far away.

Flanders Nature Center was founded in 1963 by the late artist, Natalie Van Vleck. The center is an educational organization as well as a land trust, with holdings in Woodbury, Bethlehem, Middlebury, and Southbury.

Natalie Van Vleck grew up in New York City, where she studied at the world-famous Art Students' League. As a young woman artist, she was guided by two of the most influential teachers there, Robert Henri and Max Weber. She traveled extensively to places such as the South of France, the Caribbean and Tahiti, concentrating on the bold and colorful subjects that she found in nature. In 1926, she moved to Connecticut and the focus in her art shifted to painting delicate New England wildflowers and plants and the gently rolling hills of northwestern Connecticut. After purchasing the farm in Woodbury, her interest in nature also led her to become a serious farmer, raising turkeys, sheep, and orchids on her land. She designed and worked in her art studio located near the farmhouse. Renovations on the studio were completed in 1998. It is now Flanders' administrative center as well as a welcome center for visitors.

In the summer of 1998, Flanders Nature Center, for the first time, offered art classes for children and adults. The new program "Art at the Nature Center," honors the rich artistic legacy of the center's founder by offering an opportunity for students to explore the complementary link between nature and art. For children, this is a wonderful opportunity to create paintings and drawings in an environment where the natural world is their classroom, and inspiration is found in what they see and discover while exploring nature center trails. There are also outdoor art classes for teens and adults, and a series of art-related lectures are offered in the fall.

The office and sanctuary headquarters and many of the trails are located at the Van Vleck Farm Sanctuary on Flanders and Church Hill Roads. Stop at the Studio Welcome Center and obtain a trail map before driving up Church Hill Road to the parking area. You are welcome to bring a picnic lunch as long as you carry out any refuse.

Trails on the north side of Church Hill Road take you to the sanctuary's varied habitats: a pond; woodlands, including a nut-tree arboretum; fields; wetlands; and the farm's pumpkin patch, site of a popular fall program that offers a hayride to the pumpkin patch to choose a pumpkin and listen to an educational discussion about pumpkins.

On a late summer day as I started along the Edmund Briggs Wildlife Habitat Trail, the woods were cool, a welcome refuge from the sun. From a wooden bench placed in a good position for pond viewing, I watched painted turtles sunning themselves on a log. On another occasion in June, the largest snapping turtle I have ever seen was sunning itself on a rock. The pond attracts many other species of wildlife. In the fall, migrating ducks stop to feed and rest. Farther along the trail, I stopped to watch a great blue heron. Standing in shallow water near the shore, the bird remained motionless for nearly 10 minutes before suddenly lowering its long neck and head into the pond and catching a fish. Then, with its struggling prey held securely, the heron spread its great wings and flew off across the pond. This is one method the heron uses for fishing. The other is to carefully stalk its prey as it moves along the edges of the pond in shallow water. When a frog or fish is sighted, the heron strikes quickly with its sharp beak. The heron's diet also includes insects and mice.

In addition to the pond, other sources of food attract wildlife. Fruit-bearing shrubs grow along the banks. Farther down the trail, nut trees tempt small mammals, and fields attract seed-eating birds. Not only is there food here, but shelter is also provided—even nesting boxes for wood ducks supplement the natural sites. The only sounds I heard were the calls of chickadees, catbirds, and a nuthatch, and the chattering of a red squirrel.

The Botany and Wildlife Luncheon Trails are on the south side of Church Hill Road. Plan to hike the Botany Trail during the month of May when many of the more than 100 species of wildflowers are in bloom. The trail, created in 1965, is maintained by members of the Pomperaug Valley Garden

Club of Woodbury. In addition to flowers, you will find 19 species of native ferns along this trail, plus nine species that have been introduced to the area. Be sure to look for the dark green fronds of the abundant Christmas ferns and the delicate fronds of the maidenhair ferns.

Bordering Botany Trail is Flanders Tree Farm, an eye-pleasing plantation of white spruce, Scotch pine, and blue spruce, which are being managed as Christmas trees. Bluebird nesting boxes have been placed among the spruce trees. However, providing suitable nesting sites is only half the battle in aiding the eastern bluebird. Installing baffle devices helps to prevent predators such as raccoons from getting to the nests, but in 1998, sparrows and wrens managed to appropriate most of the boxes. The season saw only one successful pair of nesting bluebirds. In contrast, the 1994 season was highly successful, with 25 fledglings raised and no losses.

In 1998, Flanders Nature Center opened a new trail, the Farm Trail, which makes use of access paths through wooded areas and new paths cut through the hay fields.

The Farm Trail, which can be accessed behind the Van Vleck farmhouse and at other points in the trail system, is a lovely walk that winds through fields, where you have a good chance of seeing bluebirds in the old apple trees, past farm buildings, beside wetlands and the pond, through wooded areas, and past the organic garden and Christmas tree farm. This trail serves as a good introduction to the rich diversity that Flanders Nature Center has to offer, from beautiful natural areas to gardens, fields, and a tree farm that demonstrate man's ability to work with nature rather than against it. On a cool, breezy, sunny day in June, it was great to walk beneath a blue sky with huge, billowing white clouds, where the sweet fragrance of wild roses filled the air, and the blossoms of yellow buttercups and red and white clover lent their color to the fields.

The Whittemore Sanctuary located in Woodbury and Middlebury consists of 684 acres that have been leased to Flanders Nature Center for more than 30 years. In June, the future of this land was uncertain because the Whittemore family had to sell the property as part of a trust agreement. The land has important ecological features, including a bog and is historically significant as one of the oldest privately managed forests in Connecticut. It includes hiking trails and Blackman's Hill, one of the highest points in the area. Hike the trail to the bog for a look at carnivorous pitcher plants as well as sundews. This trail is also great birding habitat. In spring and summer, the area is the habitat of species such as the Louisiana waterthrush and black-throated green and blackburnian warblers. In addition, green herons and wood ducks may be seen at a small woodland pond along this trail.

A haven for wildlife, this is one of the largest tracts of open land in western Connecticut. It would have been a tremendous loss to sacrifice it to development. Flanders Nature Center hoped to preserve the land as open space either through outright acquisition of the property or through a collaborative arrangement with the state or the towns.

Thanks to an appropriation from the town of Woodbury, donations from individuals and corporations, and a $450,000 state grant, by February 1999, the nature center had sufficient funds to meet the $1.3 million sales price for the land. The Whittemore Sanctuary is one of the first properties to be protected under the state's new Natural Heritage, Open Space, and Watershed Land Acquisition Grant Program.

During 1993 and 1994, an organic gardening program was developed at Flanders. Under the guidance of John Clark, owner of Clark Farms and an experienced organic gardener, adults and children can learn about soil enrichment, plant lore, insect identification and appreciation, and composting. Until 1998, the program also included farm animals that were loaned to Flanders. The goal was to create a model farm with space for plants, animals, and people. While visitors and educators loved the program, it was decided in 1998 to discontinue having farm animals and concentrate instead on organic gardening. This program continues to flourish under the leadership of John Clark. Check out the programs at Flanders on low-impact gardening, protection of water quality, soil conservation, and seed survival, edible wild plants, and butterfly and water gardens.

Throughout the year, to enhance understanding and appreciation of the natural world, Flanders Nature Center also offers many other programs for adults and children, from guided walks and lectures to an annual Fall Festival held the first weekend in October with activities for families, hayrides, games, and refreshments.

During July and August, Flanders offers nature classes at a summer day camp for children ages 4 to 12. Brochures for registration are available from the office in May.

In winter, bring your cross-country skis or snowshoes to explore the sanctuary's trails and look for animal tracks and other signs of winter wildlife.

During the month of March, you can visit Flander's maple-syrup house on Cowles Road in Woodbury, learn about the history of maple-syrup making, and watch syrup being made in the traditional way.

Where: To reach the sanctuary headquarters in Woodbury, drive north on U.S. 6, seven miles from exit 15 on I-84. Flanders Road is the second left after the intersection of State 47 and 132 (Main Street). Watch for the farmhouse and "Nature

Center" sign on your right at the intersection of Flanders and Church Hill Roads.

To reach the Whittemore Sanctuary, from I-84, proceed north on U.S. 6 (as above), but at the junction of U.S. 6 and State 64, turn right (east) on State 64 for 2.5 miles. Look for the "Flanders Nature Center" sign that marks a gravel road on the left. Turn here and drive 0.1 mile to the parking area. (Visitors should call first or stop at the Van Vleck Farm Sanctuary to pick up a trail map.)

Hours: Flanders Nature Center is open daily from dawn to dusk year-round. The office is open Monday to Saturday from 9:00 A.M. to 5:00 P.M.

Admission: Admission to the trails at the Van Vleck Farm and Whittemore Sanctuaries is free. Those who become members of Flanders Nature Center and land trust receive special discounts and the center's quarterly newsletter.

Best time to visit: Spring to see wildflowers, March to learn how maple syrup is made; but each season is special at Flanders, and any time is a good time to visit.

Activities: Birding, wildflower walks, nature study, photography, hiking, picnicking (no fires), cross-country skiing, snowshoeing, classes on art and organic gardening, nature walks, and other special programs.

For more information: Flanders Nature Center, P.O. Box 702, Woodbury, CT 06798. Call 203-263-3711.

2

Southwestern Connecticut

In a lifetime of seeing beauty in the wilderness,
I always feel a lift of spirit and an afterglow
of serenity and content.
I also know one must take time and wait
for the glimpses of beauty that always come,
and one must see each as though
it were his last chance.

—SIGURD F. OLSON
Reflections from the North Country

In southwestern Connecticut, where I have lived for 35 years, I have received many unforgettable "glimpses of beauty." Although you will not find any true wilderness areas in this part of the state, it offers many beautiful places and special wild locales where plants, birds, and other wildlife flourish.

What I remember best is the autumn foliage reflected in the mirror surface of Squantz Pond, the sight of a great blue heron feeding in a shallow area of the pond at Southford Falls State Park, the joy of glimpsing a pair of Baltimore orioles in spring at the Ansonia Nature and Recreation Center, and the combination of wild roses, dunes, and piping plovers on a sparkling morning in June at the Connecticut Audubon Coastal Center at Milford Point.

Depending on what interests you in nature, may you build your own store of enduring memories as you explore the special places of southwestern Connecticut.

Squantz Pond State Park

Surrounded by steep wooded hills, Squantz Pond State Park, four miles north of New Fairfield, is one of Connecticut's prettiest parks, especially in the fall, when the red and gold foliage of the maples and oaks is reflected in the pond's mirror surface. The pond is named for the chief of the Pootatuck Indians, who once used this area as their hunting grounds. Some years ago, a well-preserved Indian war canoe was discovered at the bottom of the pond.

In 1926, the state purchased 173 acres for the park. Land for Pootatuck State Forest, which is adjacent to the park, was acquired by the state between 1926 and 1928, thus protecting from development the entire western shore of Squantz Pond.

A natural spring-fed body of water, Squantz Pond is an arm of Candlewood Lake, one of the largest artificial bodies of water in the Northeast. The lake was created in 1926 as a power reservoir into which water from the Housatonic River was pumped from the Connecticut Light and Power Company's Rocky River Hydraulic Plant in New Milford.

Although I have visited Squantz Pond State Park several times, what stands out in my memory is one Indian-summer day in late October. Having driven to the town of Sherman near Connecticut's western border, I headed south on State 39, which follows the eastern shore of Squantz Pond. At every turn in the road, the views of the foliage and the clear blue water of the pond were spectacular.

When I reached the park, I found only a few other cars in the parking area. The sight of the long sandy beach and boat-launching area evoked memories of summers past. Squantz Pond has one of the state's most attractive swimming beaches, the surrounding hills creating the impression that you are beside a mountain lake. During the summer months, you can rent a canoe; and although the beach may be crowded on summer weekends, paddling along the pond's undeveloped western shore is still a pleasant experience.

Fall and spring are ideal for canoeing, although you must bring your own canoe with you then. I remember wishing that my canoe was not left in New Hampshire, for that Indian-summer day, with little wind, warm sun, and the display of brilliant color, would have been perfect for paddling.

The picnic area has tables and fireplaces. I had lunch at a sunny table overlooking the pond. The hills were a patchwork of red, orange, gold, and green, which contrasted with the bright blue water of the pond.

The hiking trails are on the west side of the pond. The main trail, known as the Lake Trail, is about two miles long and begins at the north end of the picnic area. I hiked this trail, which descends a hill, crosses a rustic bridge over a stream, and follows along the western shore of Squantz Pond. Here the forest reaches to the water's edge, and a rocky ridge rises from the shore of the pond to a height of more than 400 feet. An old guidebook indicates that a trail up this steep hillside led to the Council Rock of the Pootatucks and an adjoining cave. Actually, there are many caves on state-forest land and side trails leading away from the pond that can be explored. The main trail crosses two more streams before it curves to the right and ends at a small peninsula from which you get a fine view of the entire pond.

The park is a good area for seeing woodland songbirds and small mammals such as woodchucks, rabbits, red and gray squirrels, and chipmunks. The deep forests were once home to the lynx, which today in the East is found only in northern New England and extreme northern New York State. However, the rocky hills still provide sanctuary for the bobcat, which gets its name from its stubby tail.

The waters of Squantz Pond and adjoining Candlewood Lake are stocked with trout each year, so fishermen find a good supply of brown and rainbow trout as well as largemouth bass and yellow and white perch.

Squantz Pond is also one of Connecticut's parks where you can engage in winter activities. When the temperature dips well below freezing, the smooth surface of the pond provides excellent ice skating; or you may choose to spend a day in the park cross-country skiing or hiking on snowshoes.

Where: Four miles north of New Fairfield on State 39.

Hours: Open daily from 8:00 A.M. to sunset.

Admission: Parking fee during the summer season and on weekends only, from mid-April through mid-May and from Labor Day through the end of September.

Best time to visit: Spring and fall for hiking and quiet canoe trips. Summer for swimming, picnics, and canoeing. (Rental canoes are available.) To avoid crowds, visit the park on a weekday. Winter for ice skating and cross-country skiing.

Activities: Swimming, scuba diving, hiking, picnicking, fishing, boating, cross-country skiing, and ice skating. Facilities include a boat-launching ramp, modern rest rooms, a first-aid station, and drinking water.

Concessions: A food concession is in operation during the summer months. In addition, during the summer season, canoes and pedal boats are rented from North American Canoe Tours, Inc., 65 Black Point Road, Niantic, CT 06357. Call 860-739-0791.

Pets: Not allowed on the beach or near the pond. Pets on a leash allowed on wooded trails.

For more information: State Parks Division, Bureau of Outdoor Recreation, Connecticut Department of Environmental Protection, 79 Elm Street, Hartford, CT 06106-5127. Call 860-424-3200. Website: www.dep.state.ct.us.

The Elusive Bobcat

By the 1970s, the bobcat population in Connecticut had been decimated by hunters, and sightings of the animal became rare. In the mid-1970s, Connecticut began restricting hunting of bobcats, and today they are a protected species. As a result of this action, there are signs that the bobcat is making a comeback all over Connecticut.

A nocturnal animal, the bobcat spends its days in some safe hiding place such as a rock cave or thicket, where its mottled fur provides good camouflage. It is also an excellent climber. A low tree branch often serves as an observation post from which it can watch for a rabbit or mouse to pass by and provide a meal. The bobcat mates in the spring when a rock shelter, fallen tree, or hollow log may serve as the protected place it seeks for its den.

Shepaug Bald Eagle Observation Area

One of the best places to see wintering bald eagles in Connecticut is at the Shepaug Eagle Observation Area in Southbury. Northeast Utilities owns and operates this site at the Shepaug hydroelectric station on the Housatonic River.

The federally endangered bald eagle is making a comeback thanks to intensive conservation efforts. The banning of DDT and better legal protection combined with reintroduction and management efforts have led to an increase in the population.

The Shepaug Dam on the Housatonic River in Southbury attracts wintering birds because the operation of the hydro-electric station prevents the water from freezing, thus making it easy for the eagles to feed on the alewife and white perch in the river below the dam. Since the area was opened to the public in 1985, visitors come from all over Connecticut and neighboring states to observe these majestic birds. The program is managed by Northeast Utilities with volunteers from the Nature Conservancy under the guidance of the Connecticut Department of Environmental Protection.

Early on a Saturday morning in mid-February, I joined an Ansonia Nature Center field trip, led by experienced birder and avid naturalist., Tom Kilroy, to the Eagle Observation Area. We arrived at the site at 9:00 A.M. on a sunny, brisk, winter day. The best place to view the eagles is from the sturdy blind that is located near the dam. Be sure to dress warmly and bring a spotting scope if you have one. Tom set up his scope inside the blind. As many as 30 bald eagles winter in the vicinity of the Shepaug Dam, and occasionally, one has an opportunity to see the much rarer golden eagle.

We soon spotted a pair of bald eagles in the trees across the river, but they were partially hidden from view and difficult to see, even with a spotting scope. However, our attention was drawn to the field between the observation platform and the river, for the spotting scope was giving us a wonderful, up-close view of bluebirds that winter in this area and surrounding farm fields. They are also one of the nesting species that may be observed in the spring. For me, the sight of bluebirds in mid-winter was as exciting as the anticipated view of the eagles.

It was not long before we had an opportunity for a good view of a pair of bald eagles that obligingly crossed the river and perched in the trees near the dam. The chance to see these regal birds is an experience you won't forget. I can still see the pair when they took flight and soared over the observation platform. A bird of great strength and of swift and powerful flight, the distinctive white heads and tails of these adult birds were clearly visible against the clear blue of the mid-winter sky.

Bald eagle at Shepaug Bald Eagle Observation Area

Where: Westbound on I-84, take exit 14 (State 172). Go right at the bottom of the exit to the stoplight. Go left on South Main Street for one mile, crossing over the highway. Go right at the stop sign onto Fish Rock Road for one-half mile. Bear right onto River Road. Continue on River Road for more than three miles, keeping the Housatonic River on your left. Stop at the Eagle Observation Check-in Area.

Eastbound on I-84, take exit 13. Go right at the end of the exit onto Fish Rock Road. Bear right onto River Road and follow above directions.

Hours: The Eagle Observation Area is open to the public *by reservation only*, on Saturdays, Sundays, and Wednesdays from 9:00 A.M. to 1:00 P.M. from late December to mid-March. Reservations may be made beginning December 9, through a special phone line: 800-368-8954, Tuesday to Saturday from 10:00 A.M. to 4:00 P.M. (except holidays). Reservations are accepted on a first-come, first-served basis.

Admission: There is no charge.

Activities: Bird-watching and photography in winter. From Memorial Day to Labor Day, the area is open for picnicking, fishing, and nature walks. "Wildlife and Woodlore" is the theme of the nature trail.

Best time to visit: Mid-January through February is the best time to observe bald eagles. A naturalist who will help visitors spot eagles and learn about their behavior is usually at the observation station.

Pets: Pets are not permitted at the Bald Eagle Observation Area or on the grounds surrounding the area.

For more information: The Connecticut Light and Power Co., 41 Park Lane, New Milford, CT 06776. Call 860-354-8840 or Northeast Utilities (NU East, 2nd floor), Community Relations—Educational Programs, P.O. Box 270, Hartford, CT 06141-0270. Website: www.nu.com.

To make reservations for visiting the Bald Eagle Observation Area, call 800-368-8954.

During inclement winter weather, visitors are urged to call 860-665-5265 to verify whether or not the viewing area is open.

Bald Eagles in Connecticut

Not so long ago, eagles were seldom seen in Connecticut during the summer months because they did not nest in the state. Then, in 1992, for the first time in 41 years, a pair of eagles nested in Connecticut and successfully raised their young.

Bald eagles reach maturity when they are four to six years old. Pairs, which usually mate for life, begin breeding in Canada and northern New England in March and may continue into August. Courtship rituals involve spectacular aerial displays. The basket-like nest is constructed of large branches and sticks and lined with soft materials, including feathers, pine needles, grasses, and mosses. A favorite nesting site is the tallest live tree at the edge of a river or lake. The pair return to and rebuild the same nest each year. The female lays one to three dull, white eggs that hatch in approximately 35 days. Both parents take turns incubating eggs and caring for the young, which remain in the nest for 10 to 12 weeks before fledging.

Man constitutes the biggest threat to the survival of this endangered species. Today, 80 percent of all eagle deaths nationwide can be attributed to human activities, including loss of habitat due to development, disturbance of nest sites, contamination of food sources, poisoning, trapping, shooting, collision injuries, and electrocution.

Since bald eagles are easily upset, protection zones around sites of activity are maintained by federal and state personnel in cooperation with landowners. Winter feeding areas must be closely monitored because disturbances here can lead to life-threatening situations for the birds.

Southford Falls State Park

Located off State 188 in Oxford, Southford Falls State Park is an easily accessible park that is fun to visit at any season of the year. Waterfalls on the Eight Mile River, a pond that attracts waterfowl, and the possibility of seeing nesting bluebirds in the spring are just three of the reasons to visit this park.

At the turn of the century, the park was the site of the Diamond Match Company. The land, which encompasses 120 acres, was acquired by the state in 1932 after a fire destroyed the factory buildings.

On a cool, sunny day, the first weekend in October, I found the leaves just beginning to take on their autumn colors, and the pond was framed by delicate shades of red and gold foliage. Today, the name of the pond (Papermill Pond) is one of the few reminders that this was once an industrial site. Now the pond with its water plants and marshes is a haven for waterfowl. On this October day, a great blue heron was feeding in a shallow area near shore and a small flock of Canada geese was moving toward the center of the pond. The melodious honking of flocks of wild geese heading south is one sound that I always associate with autumn in New England.

The circular hiking trail skirts the shore of Papermill Pond past a wildlife marsh to an overlook. The most memorable stretch of the trail follows the Eight Mile River with its cascading falls through a deep, hemlock-lined, rocky gorge to a covered bridge. From the falls, it is just a short walk back to the parking area.

Many come to this park to fish for trout along the banks of the Eight Mile River. Kids often fish the river from the bridge near the parking area. Also near the parking lot are picnic and fishing areas accessible to people with disabilities. Other facilities include a picnic and warming shelter, rest rooms, and drinking water. Picnic sites with grills overlook the pond and the falls, making Southford Falls a favorite spot for families to come for a Sunday afternoon picnic.

On a spring bird walk, you may see nesting wood ducks in the pond; and among the returning songbirds, you can have the thrill of seeing the rare eastern bluebird. Nesting boxes have been set on poles, 8 to 12 feet above the ground in open areas. They are helping to compensate for the widespread destruction of the old apple orchards that provided this bird's favorite nesting sites.

The park is usually uncrowded, so if you are not seeking a place to swim, boat, or camp, it is a peaceful haven where you can spend a summer day by a rushing stream or among cool hemlock woods.

In winter, the park is open for ice skating, ice fishing, sledding, cross-country skiing, and snowshoeing. The park's location on a state road makes it easy to reach even in winter. It is a good place to look for winter birds or to follow animal tracks after a fresh fall of snow. The tracks of white-tailed deer, cottontail rabbits, opossums, raccoons, gray and red squirrels, and ruffed grouse are commonly seen in the winter woods.

Where: One-half mile south on State 188 from the intersection of State 67 and 188 in the village of Southford.

Hours: Daily, as conditions permit, 8:00 A.M. to sunset.

Admission: No charge.

Best time to visit: This park is not overly crowded, so any season is a good time to visit.

Activities: Hiking, picnicking, and fishing. In winter, sledding, cross-country skiing, snowshoeing, and ice fishing.

Concessions: None.

Pets: Allowed on a leash on trails and in the picnic area.

For more information: State Parks Division, Bureau of Outdoor Recreation, Connecticut Department of Environmental Protection, 79 Elm Street, Hartford, CT 06106-5127. Call 860-424-3200. Website: www.dep.state.ct.us.

Kettletown State Park

Located five miles south of Southbury, Kettletown State Park takes its name from the fact that early settlers in this area purchased a large tract of land from the Indians in exchange for one brass kettle. The park extends for about two miles along the eastern shore of Lake Zoar. The lake was created by the damming of the Housatonic River when Stevenson Dam was constructed for the purpose of obtaining hydroelectric power.

Well-spaced campsites, a sandy swimming beach, several marked hiking trails, and a Camper Nature Program during the summer months make this park a good destination for a weekend or a vacation.

The 72 partly wooded and open campsites are situated in three separate areas. When I visited the park on the first Sunday in October, only a few campers were taking advantage of the near-perfect fall weather. Doubtless, rain the previous evening had sent some of the weekend campers home. One camping area has sites in a grassy, hilly area partially shaded by maples and spruce trees. Another offers shaded sites among hemlock, oak, maple, and black-birch trees.

Camping facilities include flush toilets, showers, and a dumping station. There is an outdoor amphitheater used for nature programs and a separate campers' recreation area. Campers are allowed to use the Campground Recreation Area Shore to launch carry-in boats. Boat trailers are not allowed in the park. Trailers and RVs are limited to 26 feet in length.

The swimming beach and picnic area are located in a cove of Lake Zoar. Paugussett State Forest, which extends along the opposite shore, is a large undeveloped area for hiking, fishing, and nature study. The lake offers fishing for largemouth and smallmouth bass as well as white and yellow perch.

The Pomperaug Trail is located entirely within Kettletown State Park except for the southern end at the Jackson Cove Recreation Area. By combining this trail with the Crest Trail, a loop trip of 3.8 miles is possible. The best time to hike this trail is in June when the groves of mountain laurel are in bloom. The views of Lake Zoar are also a reason to hike this trail.

You can hike the Oxford Loop of the Pomperaug Trail as a continuation of the main trail or as a separate short hike of 1.55 miles. Parking is available at the Jackson Cove Recreation Area. The trail crosses Mill Brook, once the site of a factory that made cedar chests and other furniture. Old roads in this area descending toward the lake are a reminder that this valley was once a farming community before the construction of Stevenson Dam. Small rock caves and a waterfall on Mill Brook are two noteworthy features of this trail.

The Miller Trail, another loop of 1.55 miles, is in the northwestern section of the park, accessible from the picnic-area loop road. The trail ascends to an overlook for a bird's-eye view of Lake Zoar.

The entrance to the handicapped-accessible nature trail is off the campground road. Along this short loop trail, as well as other trails within the park, are good areas to look for woodland birds—species such as chickadees, woodpeckers, rose-breasted grosbeaks, woodland flycatchers, warblers, nuthatches, thrushes, and scarlet tanagers. Early morning and late afternoon until dusk are the best times to observe bird activity.

Where: Five miles south of Southbury, exit 15 off I-84. South on Kettletown Road for four miles, then right on George's Hill Road.

Hours: Open daily for day use from 8:00 A.M. to sunset. The campground is open from mid-April through Columbus Day. There are campsites available for rental until 10:00 P.M. each evening.

Admission: Fee for day use on weekends and holidays from Memorial Day through Labor Day weekend. There is also a nightly camping fee.

Best time to visit: The park is busiest in summer, when reservations for campsites are advisable. Spring and fall are the best times for hiking, nature study, and quiet camping.

Activities: A Camper Nature Program is offered in the summer. Swimming, hiking, camping, fishing, picnicking, nature trail, and field sports. Camping, picnicking, nature trail, and field sports are accessible to those with disabilities. Carry-in boats such as canoes may be launched by campers from the Campground Recreation Area Shore. Boat trailers not allowed in the park.

Concessions: None. Food services, laundry, etc., are available along Main Street in Southbury.

Pets: Not allowed in the campground, beach, or lake areas. Pets on a leash are permitted on hiking trails and in designated picnic areas.

For more information: For trail maps and information off-season: State Parks Division Bureau of Outdoor Recreation, Connecticut Department of Environmental Protection, 79 Elm Street, Hartford, CT 06106-5127. Call 860-424-3200. Website: www.dep.state.ct.us.

For information during the camping season: Kettletown State Park, 175 Quaker Farms Road, Southbury, CT 06488. Call the campground office, 203-264-5678; park office, 203-264-5169.

Applications for reservations are accepted, by mail only, beginning January 15 and must be received at least 10 days in advance of the intended reservation period. Camping-permit applications must be mailed directly to the campground.

Farmington Canal Linear Park and Lock 12 Historical Park

In Connecticut and elsewhere, a new type of park is being created. It is known as a linear park or greenway. In contrast to most traditional parks, linear parks are narrow belts of open space that may stretch for many miles. The segment of the Farmington Canal Linear Park in Cheshire and Hamden is an example of this type of park.

In Connecticut, the plan to transform abandoned railroad corridors and former canals into trails for hiking, bicycle riding, and open-space conservation is giving new life to the historic Farmington Canal.

In 1980, Cheshire restored a section of the old canal, making it Lock 12 Historical Park. Located off State 42, the park consists of the towpath beside the canal, lock, and lock-keeper's house as well as a helicoidal bridge, museum, and picnic area.

The museum, named after Ramon L. Beard, who did much of the early research on the history of the canal, is filled with tools and equipment that were in use at the time the canal was in operation. You can view a replica of a shovel used to start construction of the canal and a "one-horse scoop," which was the largest piece of equipment used in building the canal. Perhaps, most interesting is a framed print that depicts a team of horses moving along the towpath, hauling a barge. Close your eyes as you walk this trail, and you may hear once again the sounds of the lock being opened and the plodding of the horses' hooves along the towpath.

The Cheshire section of the Farmington Canal Heritage Trail opened in May 1994. Instead of canal boats, today's travelers go on foot, bicycle, or roller blades. The paved trail extends 2.8 miles from Cornwall Avenue to Mount Sanford Road. Parking areas are located at Lock 12 Historical Park and near the beginning of the trail at Cornwall Avenue.

Walking the trail on a weekday in early May, I found white dogwood, apple, and cherry trees in bloom. Where the trail traverses an area of wetlands, I listened to the calls of frogs and red-winged blackbirds and, at one point, saw ripples in the water and the nose of an animal that was quite possibly a muskrat. From the leafy branches of tall trees came a medley of birdsong. I spotted many robins and catbirds among the returning songbirds, as well as year-round residents such as cardinals, woodpeckers, nuthatches, and blue jays. Heading north toward Cornwall Avenue, I found mallard ducks swimming where canal boats once traveled. Houses and backyards are often visible, but along other portions of the trail, you can gaze across a hillside pasture or perhaps stop to wonder at the great variety of life in the extensive wetlands. Once an avenue of commerce, the linear park, which is maintained by the Cheshire Parks and Recreation Department, now provides area residents with a close-to-home opportunity to enjoy the outdoors.

Cheshire's Farmington Canal Linear Park is part of the Farmington Canal Heritage Trail, which, when all the towns involved have completed restoration work along the canal bed, will link New Haven, Connecticut, with Northampton, Massachusetts, via a pathway 80 miles long, extending nearly the entire length of the canal.

South of Cheshire, the town of Hamden completed construction of its northern 2.7-mile section of the trail in 1995. Extending south from the Cheshire town line to Todd Street, this part of the trail passes through an area of abundant wetlands that contain a rich variety of plants and wildlife. On a warm August afternoon, I found space in the Todd Street parking area. (On busy weekends when this small parking area is likely to be filled, you will find plenty of parking space available in Brooksvale Park at the northern end of the trail.) At Todd Street, the trail begins with a fine view of the "Sleeping Giant," a trap rock ridge formed by volcanic activity over 150 million years ago. Take time to read the information posted at the start of the trail. Written by horticulturist and Hamden resident, Andrew J. Brand, it will give you a good idea of the plants, birds, mammals, and amphibians that inhabit the moist woodlands bordering the trail. Trees include sycamore, red and sugar maples, black cherry, white ash, sumac, and red and black oak. The berries of silky and gray dogwoods provide food for birds and mammals.

More than 135 species of birds have been identified along the trail, including warblers, orioles, vireos, and flycatchers. Plan to walk the trail in May during spring migration, when flocks of 20 or 30 birds at a time are sometimes seen following the trail as they move north.

This is also one of the locations where, on an early spring evening in March, you may be able to observe the aerial song and courtship display of the male woodcock. Woodcocks nest in woodland swamps where there is a dense growth of underbrush.

Wildflower enthusiasts will also enjoy this trail. From marsh marigolds in early spring to scarlet cardinal flowers and ladies' tresses in August, the margins of the trail are home to some of our most cherished wildflowers. These, in turn, attract butterflies, including the monarch, tiger swallowtail, and the great spangled fritillary.

Many mammals are found in the surrounding woods and wetlands, including white-tailed deer, red and gray foxes, skunks, rabbits, raccoons, and muskrats. You may find the den of a red fox near the trail. The extensive wetlands are also attractive to amphibians. Snapping turtles use the soft sand of the old rail bed in which to lay their eggs. Painted turtles sun themselves on rocks or old logs, and occasionally in spring, box turtles may be observed feasting on wild strawberries.

Hamden has begun construction on the second phase of the canal trail, a 4.4-mile section that will extend the trail south to Connolly Parkway. The third phase will develop the trail to the New Haven line. South of Todd Street, the trail parallels Whitney Avenue (a main thoroughfare). By crossing Whitney Avenue and proceeding east on Mount Carmel Avenue, hikers can enter Sleeping Giant State Park with its 1,331 acres of hardwoods, hemlock ravines, ledges, and wetlands along the Mill River. The park, with 30 miles of hiking trails, is noted for woodland species of birds and also provides a good place to stop for a picnic.

The northern end of the trail, which can be accessed from Hamden's Brooksvale Park, is more remote from civilization. However, one of the amazing things demonstrated by these linear parks is the diversity of plants and wildlife to be found close to urban development. Not only do they provide a sanctuary for wildlife, but they enable people to reconnect with nature in an area near where they live.

Brooksvale Park, off Brooksvale Avenue, has two parking areas with one reserved for the trail and those who wish to visit the park's small zoo. Brooksvale Park also has a wooded picnic area with rest rooms and drinking water available.

The projected date for completion of the 14-mile section of the Farmington Canal Heritage Trail from the Southington town line to New Haven Harbor is in 2001. Meanwhile, in the northern part of the state, from Farmington to Granby, six towns are working to develop 25 miles of the trail.

Where: From the center of Cheshire, go south two miles on State 10. Turn right on State 42 (North Brooksvale Road). Lock 12 Historical Park and parking area will be on your left.

To reach the Todd Street parking area for the Hamden segment of the trail, proceed north on Whitney Avenue from the center of Hamden, and turn left on Todd Street, just past the entrance, on the right, to Sleeping Giant State Park. The parking area is on the right.

To reach Brooksvale Park, return to Whitney Avenue, turn left (north), and take your third left (Brooksvale Avenue). Brooksvale Park is on the left just before the Cheshire town line. The second parking lot is closest to the Farmington Canal Heritage Trail.

Hours: Lock 12 Historical Park is open daily March through November from 10:00 A.M. to 5:00 P.M. The Ramon L. Beard Museum is open six Sundays in the spring and six in the fall.

Tours with costumed guides are scheduled in the spring and fall. Call for information.

Farmington Canal Linear Park is open daily, sunrise to sunset.

Sleeping Giant State Park is open daily from 8:00 A.M. until sunset.

Brooksvale Park is open daily from 8:00 A.M. to one-half hour after sunset.

Admission: Admission is free to both Lock 12 Historical Park and the Farmington Canal Linear Park. At Sleeping Giant State Park, a parking fee is in effect weekends and holidays from April 1 through November 1.

Best time to visit: Any time is a good time to enjoy this trail, but birders and nature-study enthusiasts will find the early-morning hours and weekdays less crowded. Spring is the best time to see migrating birds and wildflowers. Because this is a multiuse trail, it is popular with bicyclists and in-line skaters. However, even on a Sunday afternoon, there seemed to be room for all—young and old—to enjoy the trail in their own way.

Activities: Hiking, jogging, bicycling, roller blading, bird-watching, searching for wildflowers, cross-country skiing, enjoying lunch in one of the picnic areas, and viewing the restored lock and visiting the museum in Cheshire. The trail is wheelchair accessible and is also ideally suited for pushing young children in strollers. Prohibited on the trail are motorized vehicles (other than wheelchairs), horses, and skateboards.

Pets: Dogs on a leash are allowed.

For more information: Lock 12 Historical Park, 487 North Brooksvale Road, Cheshire, CT 06410. Call 203-272-2743.

Cheshire Parks and Recreation Department, 559 South Main Street, Cheshire, CT 06410. Call 203-272-2743.

Vincent LaVorgna, Hamden Parks & Recreation, 2372 Whitney Ave., Hamden, CT 06518. Call 203-287-2669.

Connecticut Trust for Historic Preservation, 940 Whitney Avenue, Hamden, CT 06517. Call 203-562-6312.

History of the Farmington Canal

The idea to build the canal dates back to January 29, 1822, when businessmen from New Haven met with representatives from 16 other towns. Lacking the trade advantage that the Connecticut River gave to Hartford and mindful of the success of New York State's Erie Canal, they proposed building the Farmington Canal, which they envisioned as eventually connecting the St. Lawrence River with Long Island Sound. Work was started near the Massachusetts border on July 4, 1825. Engineered by Henry Farnum under the direction of James Hillhouse and Eli Whitney, the canal opened in 1828. The section that was completed ran from New Haven Harbor through Hamden, Cheshire, Southington, Plainville, Farmington, Avon, Simsbury, and Granby (all in Connecticut) to Northampton, Massachusetts, a total of 83 miles, making it the longest canal in New England. The work of building the 10-foot-wide towpath and the four-foot-deep channel for the canal, which was regulated by 28 locks to accommodate the 213-foot rise between New Haven and the Massachusetts state line, was all accomplished by men working with draft animals and simple scoops and drags. The work also involved the construction of an aqueduct over the Farmington River.

For almost 20 years, canal boats carried both freight and passengers along the waterway. However, frequent landslides made the cost of maintenance very high, resulting each year in losses for the stockholders until, in 1847, operations were suspended. In 1848, the canal was replaced by a railroad that remained in operation until 1982, when floods washed out part of the line in Cheshire.

Osbornedale State Park and the Kellogg Environmental Center

In the hills of the Naugatuck Valley, found just east of the Housatonic River in Derby and Ansonia, Osbornedale State Park covers 400 acres, a haven for many species of birds, butterflies and other wild creatures, and people. The land was once deep forest, inhabited by many species of wildlife, the hunting grounds of Paugussett Indians. European settlers began arriving in the late 1650s. They "purchased" land from the Native Americans and cleared it for farming. Its location on the Housatonic and Naugatuck Rivers led to Derby becoming an important trading port.

The park is named after the family that lived here since the mid-1800s, Major Wilbur Fisk Osborne and his wife, Ellen Lucy Davis. Wilbur was the son of John W. Osborne, the cofounder of the Osborne and Cheeseman Manufacturing Company, a brass industry in the Naugatuck Valley during the Industrial Revolution. In a time when business opportunities for women were few, their daughter, Frances, succeeded in taking over her father's business responsibilities following his death in 1907. She subsequently married Waldo Stewart Kellogg. Frances Kellogg gradually acquired numerous separate farms. Osbornedale Farms, operated by the Kelloggs, became a breeding farm for the prize-winning Osbornedale Holstein cows, and another farm was renowned as an excellent milk-producing dairy farm of Jersey cows.

Upon her death in 1956, Frances willed the 350-acre property to the people of Connecticut, preserving for future generations this large tract of undeveloped land in the highly industrialized Naugatuck Valley. The Osborne Homestead is today a museum, and with its beautiful formal gardens, is open to the public. The gardens, which include a rose garden and ornamental shrubs as well as many other perennials, were still in their prime and filled with color when I spent an afternoon there in mid-September.

Today, the park encompasses 420 acres and includes the Kellogg Environmental Center. Under the leadership of Diane Joy, a former teacher and environmental educator for the state, the center plans to expand its programs. With classroom space, the necessary educational materials, and 400 acres of fields, woods, and wetlands for field work, the Kellogg Center is just beginning to realize its potential as a center of environmental education for teachers, students, and families.

Presently, the center offers programs on nature photography, adult lectures, and workshops on topics such as composting, landscaping for birds and butterflies, and simple applications of solar energy, as well as a series of Saturday programs for families. Parents and kids can learn about nature by exploring life in a pond, searching for nesting birds, or by finding out what they can do to improve backyard habitats.

Inside the Kellogg Environmental Center building, visitors will find natural history exhibits, free informational materials, and a gift shop. Outside, on beautifully landscaped grounds, are the Butterfly and Hummingbird Garden, with flowers and nectar-filled feeding stations, and the Home Composting Demonstration Site. More than 50 species of butterflies have been identified in Osbornedale State Park, including the eastern tiger swallowtail, spicebush swallowtail, great spangled fritillary, mourning cloak, painted lady, red admiral, viceroy, and the monarch. The cultivated gardens as well as the fields and wooded areas in the park are an important habitat for butterflies, supplying both food plants for the caterpillars and nectar plants for the butterflies.

Osbornedale State Park is a great area for birding both on trails in the vicinity of the Kellogg Environmental Center and on those that can be reached from the parking area near Picketts Pond. Spring is an ideal time for bird-watching because the park's meadows, streams, and wooded hills attract 67 species of birds that are known to nest within its boundaries, including orioles, bluebirds, and red-bellied and pileated woodpeckers. Spring and fall migrations offer an opportunity to see many other species of birds as they pass through the park. In all, 177 species have been identified in Osbornedale State Park.

From the Kellogg Center parking lot, it is a short drive to the Picketts Pond area, which has a nice picnic area with tables and grills, a picturesque pond that is a favorite fishing spot for kids, hiking trails, and in case you haven't brought along a picnic lunch, a most welcome food service where you can purchase items such as hot dogs, grinders, snacks, and beverages.

The pond has a resident flock of mallards and Canada geese. Red-winged blackbirds frequent the cattails that grow along the edges of the pond, and occasionally you may see a great blue or green-backed heron. Green-backed herons nest in the park. In May, the pond area is also a good place to see migrating warblers, flycatchers, and vireos.

In winter, Picketts Pond becomes a favorite destination for ice skating, with night lighting and a warm-up hut provided.

Park trails can also be enjoyed when there is sufficient snow cover for cross-country skiing and snowshoeing. It's a good place to look for winter birds and tracks of native wildlife, including deer, wild turkeys, raccoons, and foxes.

Where: Osborne Homestead Museum and the Kellogg Environmental Center: From State 34 (Main Street) in Derby, continue west on State 34 for about 1.5 miles. Turn right on Cedric Avenue, then left onto Hawthorne Avenue at the T intersection. Parking is about 200 feet on the left.

Picketts Pond Area of Osbornedale State Park: Leaving the Kellogg Environmental Center, turn right on Hawthorne Avenue. After 0.6 mile, turn left on Chatfield Street. The park entrance is 0.4 mile on the left. There is parking by the picnic area near the pond.

Hours: Osbornedale State Park is open daily from 8:00 A.M. until sunset year-round as conditions permit.

The Kellogg Environmental Center is open Tuesday through Saturday, 9:00 A.M. to 4:30 P.M.

The Osborne Homestead Museum is open from May until mid-December. Guided tours are available Saturday and Sunday from 10:00 A.M. to 4:00 P.M., and Thursday from 10:00 A.M. to 3:00 P.M. In December, a week of special holiday tours is offered.

Admission: There is no charge for admission to Osbornedale State Park, the Kellogg Environmental Center, or the Osborne Homestead formal gardens. Registration is required for all programs at the Kellogg Environmental Center. A fee is charged for some programs. Donations are requested on tours of the Osborne Homestead Museum to help defray expenses.

Best time to visit: Spring and fall for birding. Summer for butterfly walks. Winter for ice skating, cross-country skiing, and snowshoeing.

Activities: Birding and nature study, hiking, photography, environmental programs and nature walks, tour of the gardens and museum, picnicking, fishing, cross-country skiing, ice skating, and snowshoeing.

Concessions: A food concession is open near Picketts Pond from April to October.

Pets: Permitted on a leash on hiking trails in Osbornedale State Park.

Other: Covered picnic pavilions, with fireplaces and picnic tables inside the building that houses the food concession, provide shelter in inclement or cold weather.

Trail maps are available at the Kellogg Environmental Center.

For more information: State Parks Division, Bureau of Outdoor Recreation, Department of Environmental Protection, 79 Elm Street, Hartford, CT 06106-5127. Call 860-424-3200. Website: www.dep.state.ct.us.

Kellogg Environmental Center (or Osborne Homestead Museum), P.O. Box 435, 500 Hawthorne Avenue, Derby, CT 06418. Call 203-734-2513 (for additional information or to register for any programs).

Connecticut Amphibian Monitoring Project

For more than a decade, scientists have been concerned about the apparent decline of many amphibian populations in Europe, Australia, and North and South America.

The Connecticut Amphibian Monitoring Project (CAMP) is the result of interested staff from several environmental and educational organizations in Connecticut who worked to organize a volunteer-based amphibian monitoring program.

Launched in the spring of 1998, CAMP's 15-year mission is to study the changes in amphibian life that may eventually affect all vertebrates, including human beings. Volunteers, under the guidance of environmental educators, are collecting long-term scientific data on Connecticut's amphibian populations. The second goal of this project is to increase public awareness of amphibian populations and the need for conservation and habitat protection.

There is a special concern about malformed frogs that have been discovered in many locations around the world, including Connecticut. Like the canary in the coal mine, it is believed that amphibians may be an indicator species for mankind. If amphibians are not doing well, it is important to find out what environmental changes are threatening them and may ultimately threaten humans.

In Connecticut, there are twelve study blocks so that anyone interested in CAMP should be able to find a study area near his or her hometown.

Staff at the Kellogg Environmental Center and the Ansonia Nature Center have joined together to direct the research project in the Great Hill Section of Ansonia, Derby, and Seymour. During the spring, summer, and fall of 1998, participants counted amphibians, including frogs, toads, newts, and salamanders, and recorded their observations and other information such as weather conditions and description of land use on standard data sheets.

For more information: Contact Hank Gruner, Science Center of Connecticut, 950 Trout Brook Drive, West Hartford, CT 06119-1437. Call 860-231-2824.

For information on the Great Hill survey block, call Roger Lawson, lead program specialist for the Kellogg Environmental Center, 203-734-2513, or Donna Lindgren, director, at the Ansonia Nature and Recreation Center, 203-736-9360.

Lower Naugatuck River

A warm, sunny Indian-summer day in October found a group of us participating in a canoe trip organized by the Ansonia Nature Center, the Naugatuck Chapter of Trout Unlimited, and John Kulick, our outfitter and the owner of Huck Finn Adventures in Collinsville, Connecticut.

It was an almost idyllic float trip. Our launch site was in Ansonia about one-fourth mile below the Ansonia Copper and Brass Company. As our flotilla of eight canoes headed downstream, paddling was effortless, and there was time for bird-watching, photography, and enjoying the fall foliage along the east bank of the river.

"To naturalists, the Naugatuck River is one of the best places for birds," Donna Lindgren, director of the Ansonia Nature Center, had told our group. We watched several great blue herons that were fishing the river and paused several times to look at ducks and double-crested cormorants flying overhead. Later, we were to see a great egret near the water's edge, its snowy white plumage illuminated by the afternoon sun. Both common and red-throated loons are also seen on the river during migration periods.

What is memorable about this trip is not just that it was a great way to see birds and to spend a perfect fall day, but that we were celebrating the rebirth of a river.

After two miles of leisurely paddling downstream, we reached the confluence of the Naugatuck and Housatonic Rivers and our takeout destination on O'Sullivan's Island in Derby. The island's sandy shore was a welcome sight after our difficult launching, which required carrying the canoes down a steep bank covered with loose rocks, the result of a flood control project by the U.S. Army Corps of Engineers after the 1955 flood.

It is best to avoid canoeing into the Housatonic River where a strong tidal current and heavy powerboat traffic can make it dangerous to be in a small boat.

As we ended our canoe trip, we were excited by the sight of so many birds and the realization that the Naugatuck has the potential to once again be a wild and scenic river. The Naugatuck is an important migratory corridor, part of the Atlantic Flyway, ensuring that bird-watching is especially rewarding during spring and fall migrations.

What is happening here is not unique to Connecticut. Today, people canoe, swim, and fish in New England rivers that were once badly polluted waters, but it is exciting to witness the rebirth of a river and wonderfully encouraging to know that if life can return to Connecticut's most polluted river, there is hope for rivers and streams all over New England.

Where: A donation of 8.3 acres of land bordering the river by Complete Construction to the city of Ansonia for open space and conservation purposes should ensure public access for canoeing at least by the year 2000. The Kinneytown Dam in Seymour is another possible launch site. At the present time, an outfitter leading a river trip must obtain permission to access the river from local landowners.

Hours: Because the lower Naugatuck River is tidal, it is best to plan a canoe trip to coincide with the time of high tide.

Fees: Cost of canoe rentals from Huck Finn Adventures varies, depending on the number of canoes rented, and includes all equipment, a shuttle, and excellent service.

Best time to plan a canoe trip: Spring and fall during migration periods are the best times to see wildlife along the river. It is recommended that anyone interested in a float trip on the lower Naugatuck contact an organization that has had experience planning canoe trips or an outfitter who knows the river. Also, scout the river just prior to the trip. Heavy rain can produce widely fluctuating water conditions. While our trip turned out to be a leisurely paddle suitable for canoeists with limited experience, higher or lower water conditions can cause problems. In addition, the best time to plan a canoe trip will be after Waterbury completes the upgrade to its sewer plant, which should be in the spring of 2000. Prior to that time, avoid contact with the river water as much as possible or take a shower if you are accidentally exposed to it.

Activities: Canoeing, birding, and other wildlife watching, fishing, and photography.

For more information: The Ansonia Nature and Recreation Center, 10 Deerfield Road, Ansonia, CT 60401. Call 203-736-9360 for information on the Naugatuck River and a schedule of planned events that may include a canoe trip on the river.

John Kulick, Huck Finn Adventures, Inc., P.O. Box 137, Collinsville, CT 06022. Call 860-693-0385. (John has had experience canoeing the upper Naugatuck River, which is a white-water trip, as well as the lower river.)

For information on the restoration of the Naugatuck River, for information on the Naugatuck Chapter of Trout Unlimited, or to get involved with the watchdog program, call Trout Unlimited at 203-264-1976 or Jon Ploski at 203-881-5030.

Rebirth of a River

Native Americans knew the Naugatuck and its valley as a beautiful wild river teeming with fish and other wildlife. Decades ago, the river and O'Sullivan's Island at the confluence of the Housatonic and Naugatuck Rivers were still popular recreation sites for valley residents. However, for many years, the Naugatuck was really only valued for its waterpower and as a disposal site for industries that built along its banks. By the 1970s, this devastating course of action had taken its toll. The Naugatuck was too polluted south of West Torrington to support aquatic life.

Albin Weber, president of the Naugatuck Chapter of Trout Unlimited, credits three factors with saving the Naugatuck. The first was the disastrous flood of 1955. The cause of great suffering and hardship for valley residents, the flood, nevertheless, had a beneficial effect on the river, for it wiped out most of the polluting industries and their dams. Second, the 1972 Clean Water Act, passed by the federal government, set in motion the procedure for upgrading the nation's sewage treatment facilities to meet federal standards. Following the 1955 flood, pollution from industry was no longer a major factor. The main source of pollution now was from the inadequate sewage treatment plants in towns along the river. By 1998, most towns had upgraded their plants to meet federal standards. In fact, the towns of Seymour and Beacon Falls have state-of-the-art facilities. Only the city of Waterbury is still working to upgrade its plant.

The third factor that Weber considers important in bringing about the rebirth of the Naugatuck River is the fact that once all life in the river had been destroyed and it became ugly and polluted, the towns turned their backs on the river. They built walls, trying to shut the river out of their lives. Yet, this negative action had a positive result. Without constant interference, it gave nature time to begin the healing process. In spite of some continuing sources of pollution, the river began to clean itself. Today, the fish population has been reestablished and the chain of life rebuilt, as signified by the return to the river of osprey, bald eagles, herons, kingfishers, muskrat, mink, and other wildlife.

Our canoe trip proved to be a newsworthy event for the local papers, for it is only recently that the valley towns have begun to focus their attention on bringing people back to the rivers. Both the Naugatuck and the Housatonic Rivers have great potential as sources of renewal and recreation for all who live in or visit this area of southwestern Connecticut, and since the river water eventually flows into Long Island Sound, cleaning up the rivers plays a significant role in the effort to restore Long Island Sound.

A number of exciting projects, which will make the Naugatuck once again accessible to hikers, canoeists, birders, and other wildlife watchers, are underway. As part of the Naugatuck River gateway initiative, the town of Beacon Falls has completed a timber staircase on the east side of the river, leading from the Senior Citizens Center on North Main Street down to the river with a patio along the waterfront.

Meanwhile, on the west bank of the river, O&G Industries, Inc., which owns a quarry downstream, is building a riverside trail from its property south to the Seymour town line. In other valley towns, the riverside trail is in the planning stage and envisioned for the future is a greenway trail that will extend from the Massachusetts border to Long Island Sound along the banks of the Naugatuck and Housatonic Rivers.

Seven of the Naugatuck's eight remaining dams are scheduled for demolition. In 1998, construction was begun on a fish ladder at the remaining Kinneytown Dam in Seymour and on another at the former site of the Tingue Mill Dam in Seymour, where a natural waterfall remains. This action, undertaken by the Department of Environmental Protection, will enable salmon and other kinds of migratory fish to once again swim upstream to their ancestral spawning grounds. The restocking of the river with shad and herring benefits not only those who like to fish, but birds of prey and other wildlife for whom these fish are a main food source.

The projected date for the completion of Waterbury's sewer plant and the fish-ladder installation program is the year 2000. This will remove the last major obstacle to water purity along the river and to the rebirth of a natural ecosystem.

One evening, following our canoe trip, I had an opportunity to visit the site in Ansonia where 8.3 acres of land bordering the river is being donated to the city. Standing on the flood plain of the river just before sunset, gazing at the orange and gold foliage of the wooded area along the west bank, I had mixed emotions about this visit. On the one hand, I was glad that at least a small part of this 58-acre tract of land would be preserved and that the citizens of Ansonia would finally have access to their river, but at the same time, I was dismayed that this last remaining parcel of land with mature forest that had been growing for nearly a century, a haven for both people and wildlife, was soon to be developed.

A gently sloping shoreline provides an ideal location to launch canoes. By the water's edge, we spotted many animal tracks— deer, muskrat, and raccoons as well as tiny paw prints left by a small mammal.

The Naugatuck Chapter of Trout Unlimited and its River Keepers led by Dave Hull adopted as their project the restoration of the Naugatuck River. They have cleaned up the river and acted as river guards to help ensure that regulations are followed. In December 1998, Jon M. Ploski, a watershed reclamation specialist, was appointed by Trout Unlimited and MacDermid, Inc., of Waterbury as the first full-time "River Steward" for the Naugatuck. Ploski's job is to act as an environmental watchdog for the river and to supervise watershed restoration efforts for Trout Unlimited. As Albin Weber says, "Someone has to be a voice for the river, and when people focus on the river, it's amazing what can be accomplished."

Ansonia Nature and Recreation Center

The citizens of Ansonia can be proud of their nature center. It is one of only two environmental centers that serve the towns of the Naugatuck Valley. The other is the Kellogg Environmental Center in Derby. Situated on 104 acres that encompass fields, woods, a pond, and wetlands, the location of the nature center is remembered as the site of one of the last operating dairy farms in Ansonia. Whenever I walk the trail along the old wagon road (Milan Road) in the late afternoon, I recall Angelo Ferla, whose family owned the farm from 1915 until 1938, telling me that one of his favorite boyhood memories is of bringing the cows home from the high pasture reached by this wagon road.

The Ansonia Nature and Recreation Center is a city-owned park. On November 19, 1977, the park was dedicated to the citizens of Ansonia. For most of those years, since November 1979, Donna Lindgren has been the center's executive director. A creative and dedicated leader, she has guided the center's development through the years, working to help the nature center fulfill its mission—"to instill a reverence for all life and to promote a lasting environmental stewardship of the earth." With support from a small staff, family, and other volunteers, including the "Friends of the Ansonia Nature Center," Donna has developed exhibits and a schedule of environmental programs that include nature walks, special programs and workshops, and holiday celebrations for families as well as programs for children, including "Summer Nature Days" and a Junior Ranger Program. In addition, the Ansonia Nature Center offers a schedule of seasonal programs for school children. Hundreds of children come to the center each year for classes taught by Donna; Alison Stowe, assistant director; or any of the other enthusiastic part-time rangers. One has only to sit in on a class Donna or Alison is teaching to understand that each makes learning about the natural world exciting and fun.

The main building houses an exhibit area, a small nature library, nature shop, space for classrooms and meetings, and live animal exhibits, as well as the animal rehabilitation center. Many kids head for the aquarium room for a close-up view of turtles, snakes, frogs, and lizards. Although the center's main focus is on native wildlife, several domestic animals, including Mocha, the rabbit, have found a home at the nature center and a place in the educational programs as well as in the hearts of local children and staff.

Most permanent residents at the center are like the great horned owl, "Hooter," who cannot be released back into the wild. Hooter's collision with an automobile robbed him of his ability to fly, and his "home" must now be an enclosed area, just outside the nature center building. Most of us who work with wildlife have mixed feelings about a wild creature that must remain in captivity, yet Hooter's presence at the nature center helps children learn about owls and other birds of prey. Sometimes at night, I am told by members of the staff, when all is quiet, they have heard Hooter's low, sonorous call, "hoo, hoo hoo, hoo, hoo," breaking the stillness of the night.

Two big brown bats also reside at the nature center. These bats were hand-reared by a well-intentioned person. Unfortunately, their human caretaker could not teach them what they need to know to survive in the wild. Having always been hand-fed, they have no idea how to hunt for food. Actually, it is illegal in Connecticut to care for most wild birds and animals unless you are a licensed rehabilitator.

There are almost 1,000 species of bats in the world, but only 8 are found in Connecticut, including the rare Indiana bat. The two most common bats in Connecticut are the little brown bat and the big brown bat. Bats are furred, warm-blooded mammals. They have good eyesight, but for navigation and catching prey at night, they rely on echolocation.

Bats are probably one of our most misunderstood mammals. Attending one of the nature center's programs on bats is a good way to learn about these highly beneficial mammals and dispel any false beliefs that you may have about these wild creatures. Connecticut's bats are primarily insect eaters. As the only major predators of night-flying insects, they consume many garden and other pests, including cutworms, potato beetles, corn borer moths, and mosquitoes.

Bats need our help to survive. Loss of older trees and abandoned barns has deprived bats of many of the good roosts they used in the past. At the Ansonia Nature Center, you can learn how to make "bat boxes" or purchase one in the nature shop. The bat boxes are only one example of what individuals can do to help wildlife survive by providing alternative shelters. Another way we can help bats is to discourage the use of insecticides that not only harm bats directly, but destroy the insects they depend on for food.

Wild Bird and Animal Rehabilitation Program

Donna Lindgren is also a licensed wildlife rehabilitator. Under her direction and with the help of staff and volunteers, most of whom are also licensed rehabilitators, the Ansonia Nature Center is playing an increasingly important role as a rehabilitation facility for orphaned and injured birds and animals. In 1998, about 450 birds and animals were cared for. During the past 10 years, the center has nursed many species of birds back to health and raised innumerable abandoned young birds that would have otherwise perished. Those especially remembered by staff include four baby screech owls, three fledgling red-bellied woodpeckers, bluebirds, an eastern ruby-crowned kinglet, a common loon, a great blue heron, a turkey vulture, cardinals, and a Carolina wren. Gray, red, and flying squirrels; chipmunks; rabbits; and opossums have also received care at the center or in the home of a wildlife rehabilitator. As a volunteer, I have had an opportunity to help with the feeding and care of the wild birds and mammals. Unfortunately, there are many injured birds and animals for whom no help is possible other than euthanasia to end their pain. Most of these are victims of attacks by domestic cats and dogs. Responsible pet ownership that includes keeping dogs on a leash and cats inside (or, at least, closely supervised, if allowed to go outside), can do much to reduce the needless destruction of wildlife.

Those interested in wildlife are anxious to help an injured or orphaned bird or animal. However, removing a wild creature from its natural surroundings is a drastic step that may not have a happy ending. If the creature is injured, there may be little choice, but if you find a baby bird or animal alone, chances are good that the parent is nearby and will return to care for its offspring if you don't interfere.

On November 15, 1997, many of those who attended the 20th Anniversary Celebration at the Ansonia Nature and Recreation Center had a rare opportunity to watch the release of a red-throated loon on the nature center pond. The loon, which had been following the Naugatuck River, had been brought to the center the previous day during an ice storm after it mistook an Ansonia parking lot for open water. Normally, a red-throated loon takes flight by rising and running along the surface of the water for a distance of 50 to 130 feet until it reaches the speed necessary for takeoff. In good condition, the loon at the nature center needed only the surface of the pond to enable it to take flight and resume its migration toward warmer coastal waters. As I stood on the shore of the pond on that wintery afternoon, watching the red-throated loon, I understood why wildlife rehabilitators say being able to release a bird or animal back into the wild makes all the hard work and disappointments worthwhile.

Birding on Nature Center Trails

The Ansonia Nature and Recreation Center has two-and-a-half miles of trails. Because of its diverse habitats, it is home to many species of wildlife. A walk on these trails can be a fascinating experience at any season of the year. In the nature center building, you can pick up a trail map that shows the primary circular nature trail and the network of secondary trails that connect to it. These trails take you along the shore of the pond where you are likely to see mallards. Listen for the calls of red-winged blackbirds as you climb the hill through the fields into the woods. Old stone walls and fields are reminders that this was once farmland. In the spring, look for bluebirds and wood ducks. Nesting boxes have been provided for both species. Baltimore orioles and scarlet tanagers are among the rarer species that are known to nest at the nature center. Indigo buntings are occasionally sighted in the area, and a spring or fall walk can provide an exciting opportunity to see migrating warblers. If you want to learn more about birds, join one of the early morning bird walks held the second Saturday of each month, year-round.

Talk with Donna Lindgren about songbirds, and you will understand why she and other scientists are deeply concerned about neotropical migrants, birds including warblers, swallows, vireos, orioles, scarlet tanagers, and robins that each year travel to and from South and Central America. These birds are in deep trouble due to destruction of habitat through overdevelopment in America. Each year, fewer migratory warblers and wood thrushes are seen in Connecticut, and the song of the meadowlark is seldom heard these days.

It is thought that the key to preventing further decline in our songbird population lies in managing large natural areas in a way that makes them attractive to birds. Linear parks, which link together smaller parks and preserves, can also help to combat the fragmentation of the landscape caused by overdevelopment, which may be as damaging to migrating birds as the destruction of the tropical rain forests in South America.

Spring Wildflower Walk

Another favorite trail is a self-guiding nature trail with a boardwalk through woods and wetlands where wildflowers and ferns grow in the shaded humus-rich soil. I remember a spring wildflower walk in early May led by Donna, whose love of wildflowers goes back to her childhood. The nature center has native fern and wildflower gardens as well as a butterfly garden. We started out by the cultivated garden where Donna identified an ostrich fern regarded by many as the handsomest of our eastern ferns. It can grow to a height of seven feet. Here, too, you will find wild ginger, sensitive ferns, yellow violets, maidenhair ferns, red and white trillium, wood anemones, and a beautiful yellow slipper orchid that flowers later in the spring.

Leaving the wildflower garden, we headed for the self-guiding nature trail where Solomon's seal, Canada mayflower, and the lovely rose blooms of the wild geranium flourish in the woodland soil. The Canada mayflower berries, Donna told us, are edible with a tart taste. To the right of the boardwalk that crosses a wetland area, we found sweet pepperbush. This hardy, native shrub is known for its fragrant white flowers that bloom in early August. The flowers are followed by clusters of small, brown seed pods that remain on the plant during the winter, providing food for birds and other wildlife. Here in this wet area with its vernal pools, there once was a beautiful display of cardinal flowers. Their red blooms no longer light up the dark woods, and no one can explain what happened to this plant. Yet, as Donna pointed out, "one of the delightful qualities of wildflowers is their ephemeral nature." Even when you walk the same trail each spring, it becomes an exciting adventure because you never know what wildflower may suddenly appear in a given location, or what familiar plants may have vanished from an area.

Dwarf ginseng and wood anemones were in bloom. The leaves of these two tiny plants, which both grow in moist woods, are similar but each has a distinctive white bloom that makes the plant easy to identify by its flowers or seed pods. Two varieties of purple violets were in bloom, and on top of a hill, where there is a picnic grove and drier ground, we spotted a lovely patch of bluets, which Donna remembers her mother called quaker-ladies.

Spicebush is another native shrub that is found in abundance along the edge of the woods. This shrub is easily identified by its aromatic fragrance if you scratch the bark or crush the leaves, and its shiny red berries are a favorite food of fruit-eating birds.

Other wildflowers of special interest that you may see on a spring walk include the lovely pink moccasin flower or lady's slipper, one of Connecticut's native wild orchids; marsh marigolds, whose bright yellow blooms are a wonderful tonic for the soul tired of drab winter days; and trout lilies, named for their mottled leaves that resemble the backs of brook trout.

Although the day of our walk was cloudy, and the woods wet from a morning shower, what I remember from that day is the excitement of finding certain wildflowers we did not expect to see along with the delicate blooms of the wild pink azaleas and the varying shades of new green foliage that transformed this forested area into a woodland garden.

Tracking Wildlife in Winter

Al LePri has been a part-time ranger at the nature center for the past eight years. A born naturalist, Al is the leader of the Junior Rangers Program, conducts many of the hikes and nature walks for families, and helps teach the nature classes for children. Raptors are his special interest, a concern that grew out of his experience working at a raptor rehabilitation center in New Mexico. I recall a late December, Sunday afternoon hike at the nature center led by Al. It was a day of brilliant sunshine with a couple of inches of fresh, powdery snow that had fallen during the night. A group of about 30 adults and children participated in the 90-minute hike through the woods and fields. Al prefers winter hikes on snow-covered ground when animal tracks are a lot more visible. On this particular day, the tracks of cross-country skiers had obliterated animal tracks that might have been visible early that morning, but we did find tracks that were most likely made by a red fox. Like all members of the canine family, the claws are prominent, but the track is more delicate than other members of this group. Look for small pad impressions that are widely spaced and a trail that is almost a straight line. We also found tracks of white-tailed deer and discovered where they had fed on the branches and bark of the red cedar trees, a favorite winter food in this area of New England. Other tracks that you might discover on a winter walk include those made by coyotes, rabbits, opossums, squirrels, and wild turkeys.

Maple Syrup Workshop

One of the most popular programs for families is the Maple Syrup Workshop, held each year in March. Native Americans started the tradition of making maple syrup many centuries ago. Each year when the sap is running, nature center staff carry on that tradition. Participants learn how to identify which trees to tap and how to make their own spiles. Then, they gather around the fireplace in the picnic pavilion, and watch as the collected sap is boiled over an open fire. The best part comes last when the sap has boiled down and everybody gets to taste this delectable New England treat poured over ice cream.

For the Future

Overlooking the pond near the community gardens, a new building, the Redwing Pond House, is nearing completion. It will house an environmental learning center for preschool children and include living quarters for a resident naturalist intern.

Nature center staff are hoping the city of Ansonia will purchase an adjoining 45-acre, forested tract of land, which is being offered for sale by Birmingham Utilities of Ansonia. The acquisition of this land and its preservation as open space for the benefit of wildlife and man is seen as being of the highest priority in order to ensure a corridor for wildlife, prevent further fragmentation of the landscape, and prevent the nature center lands from becoming an island in a sea of housing and commercial developments.

Citizen groups and The Trust for Public Land are also working to ensure the preservation of an additional 613 acres of utility-owned land in Ansonia and Seymour that would otherwise be sold to a developer.

The state, through its Recreation and Natural Heritage Trust Program, has indicated an interest in preserving this forested land as open space, but municipal funding will also be needed if this land is to be protected.

Where: From the intersection of State 115 and 243 in Ansonia, follow 243 east. Turn left (north) on Benz Street. Bear right on Milan Road, and left on Deerfield Road.

Hours: The park is open daily, dawn to dusk, year-round. The nature center building is open daily, year-round, except on major holidays, from 9:00 A.M. to 7:00 P.M. (9:00 A.M. to 5:00 P.M. during winter months).

Admission: No admission charge, but visitors may wish to join or donate to the Friends of the Ansonia Nature Center, Inc., and help support the center's programs.

Best time to visit: Spring to see birds and wildflowers; fall for foliage walks, hikes in search of wild mushrooms, and to see migrating birds; winter for cross-country skiing, snowshoeing, ice skating, and tracking wildlife; summer for nature walks and picnics.

Activities: Birding, wildflowers walks, nature photography, hiking, fishing, playground and athletic fields, picnicking, cross-country skiing, snowshoeing, skating, exhibits, and special programs for families; nature walks and natural history classes for children. A calendar of events is available. Also gardening. For a small fee, a plot may be rented in the Community Gardens. Group camping is by special permit only, in designated areas.

Bicycles, horses, snowmobiles, and other motorized vehicles are not allowed on the trails.

Pets: All pets must be on a leash.

For more information: Ansonia Nature and Recreation Center, 10 Deerfield Road, Ansonia, CT 06401. Call 203-736-9360. Website: www.invalley.org/ansonia/nature.

Biodiversity Monitoring Project

One of the most exciting events to occur at the Ansonia Nature and Recreation Center was the start on June 8, 1998, of a Biodiversity Monitoring Project, when 42 students from Derby Middle School, Derby High School, and Wooster Middle School in Stratford began a field study on a selected hectare of land that has remained relatively undisturbed for the last 75 years. The world-wide monitoring project, headed by the Smithsonian Institution in Washington, began in nations around the world several years ago and is intended to record plant and animal life in different regions so that the effects of natural and human interventions can be measured. Connecticut is the first state in the United States to involve students in the project.

After attending a special workshop conducted in Southbury by the Smithsonian and Southern Connecticut State University, director Donna Lindgren presented the program to the Ansonia Board of Education in January 1998, and the following month to a group of teachers.

"This project will provide students and their teachers an opportunity to be involved in an exciting research project, one of only a handful of such projects underway in the United States," Donna explains. "It will give students the know-how to monitor, measure, and access our own biodiversity, which should result in a new level of local environmental awareness. . . . The development of a species list for the site and the ability to monitor the site over a period of years should provide important and needed information about wildlife in our own community."

On December 1, 1998, I had an opportunity to talk with Ed Kulikowski, a technology teacher at Wooster Middle School in Stratford, when he brought 21 eighth-grade students to spend a day working on the biodiversity monitoring project. Most were there for the second time. The teens, nearly all students in gifted programs, had chosen to work on this project. They had started by identifying the trees in the plot and measuring their diameters and heights. That day, they were placing metal tags on all the trees with a diameter of four centimeters or more.

Ed Kulikowski also attended the workshop in Southbury and has been appointed the New England regional director for biodiversity by the Smithsonian Institution. He sees this project as having a far-reaching effect on students. "It changes all of their attitudes about the environment," he says. "They become better stewards of the land, both locally and globally."

Talk with the students and you'll find that they're enthusiastic about being part of the project. "If we learn more about our country, we'll take better care of it," Kyle tells me. Kelly is excited about going to Washington, D.C., where they'll meet students from Canada who are also participating in the project. Kara has decided she wants to be an environmentalist. Dawn says, "It's fun to learn how society affects the environment," and Sarah, "It's cool that we're working with the environment." Many echo Alden's thoughts: "I think it's great that they're letting middle-school students do scientific research!"

If all goes well with the project, other plant life will be monitored, including wildflowers, ferns, and fungi. The study of birds, amphibians, reptiles, arthropods, and mammals will follow.

Watching these teens at work makes you feel hopeful about the future of our planet. Ed Kulikowski expresses it best: "If you can empower these students now, they will be able to take control later and make more enlightened decisions about their environment and its relationship to their community."

For more information: Adults, students, or groups who would like to get involved with the Ansonia Nature Center's biodiversity project can call Donna Lindgren at 203-736-9360.

Connecticut Audubon Coastal Center and Stewart B. McKinney National Wildlife Refuge

One of the best areas in Connecticut to see shore and water birds is the Connecticut Audubon Coastal Center at Milford Point. Opened in 1995, the coastal center is located on an 8.4-acre barrier beach known as the Smith-Hubbell Wildlife Refuge, an area that has been known to birders since the 1930s. It adjoins the 840-acre Wheeler Wildlife Management Area, a salt marsh at the mouth of the Housatonic River. A short walk west along the shoreline leads to the Milford Point Unit of the Stewart B. McKinney National Wildlife Refuge. An observation deck at the entrance to the refuge offers visitors an overview of the salt marsh, mudflats, ocean, and barrier beach at the mouth of the Housatonic River. Here, waterfowl, shorebirds, and wading birds find a safe haven to feed and rest during their long spring and fall migrations. Over 50 species of waterfowl, shore birds, and wading birds have been observed during migration periods.

Spring and fall are also the most exciting times to be at the Smith-Hubbell Wildlife Sanctuary, where more than 230 species of birds have been recorded in the area. In a heavily populated section of the southwestern coast of Connecticut, this area of marsh and barrier beach on Long Island Sound has fortunately been preserved for wildlife.

When I visited the sanctuary in the spring of 1994, construction work on the coastal center had not yet begun, but a restoration project sponsored by the Connecticut Audubon Society, the New Haven Bird Club, and the Department of Environmental Protection was nearly complete. The project included the construction of a boardwalk over the low dune area leading to the beach and benches on an observation platform that provide a wonderful spot to sit and scan the edge of the tide and the offshore barrier beaches for birds. The restoration effort also involved the removal of invasive plant species and the replanting of native species designed to provide an improved habitat for wildlife. Today, wild roses bloom in early June, transforming what was once a rather barren area into a place of beauty as well as a haven for wildlife.

Smith-Hubbell is a sanctuary for two of Connecticut's threatened species of birds—the piping plover and the least tern. Fencing helps protect the low dune area, the nesting ground of the piping plover, a pale sand-colored bird with orange legs and a black, yellow-tipped bill. A single neckband also helps identify this bird. Arriving in March, the birds seek an isolated sandy beach with sparse vegetation for their nesting grounds. They must also have access to mudflats for feeding. In late April, the first eggs are laid in a shallow depression in the sand, often lined with shell fragments and placed near vegetation. The three or four eggs, which are cream-colored with dark brown flecks, hatch in 27 days. The chicks, which leave the nest within hours of hatching, are very vulnerable to beach traffic and predators. As I watched several adult plovers feeding at the edge of the tide, I heard their whistled call of "peep-lo."

The least tern is a gull-like bird about the size of a robin. Its long-pointed wings have a span of about 20 inches, and its tail is forked. It has a gray back, white belly, white forehead with a black cap, black wingtips, and yellow feet and bill. Arriving in early May, least terns form pairs that stay together the whole season. They prefer broad, sandy, vegetation-free beaches located close to an estuary with an abundant supply of food. Here the two small offshore barrier beaches serve as the nesting grounds for the least terns. In mid-May, the first eggs are laid in a shallow depression in the sand. The nests have one to three cream-colored eggs with dark brown blotches. The eggs hatch in 21 days, and the young leave the nest by the second day. By the 23rd day, they are able to fly but continue to be fed by the parents until migration.

Several factors have led to the decline in numbers of both these species in Connecticut. Shoreline development has limited the availability of suitable nesting sites, and recent beach-stabilization projects have reduced the quality of the remaining sites. The birds are forced to use areas with more vegetation, which gives cover to predators like dogs, cats, rats, raccoons, and skunks. Human disturbance, which can include outright nest destruction, is also a factor. When visiting the refuge—or any beach area—during nesting season, from April 1 to September 1, it is extremely important to keep away from the nesting areas. Disturbing the birds prevents them from attending to their nests and young. If dogs are allowed on the beach, they should be kept on a leash at all times. In addition, food scraps that might attract predators should not be left on the beach.

On the other side of the refuge, near the parking area, a new observation platform provides a good view of the extensive marshes that are part of the 840-acre Charles E. Wheeler Wildlife Management Area. Consisting of Nell's Island and the surrounding salt marsh, the management area is named after local conservationist and well-known decoy carver, Charles "Shang" Wheeler, who in the 1930s was instrumental in protecting this area from development.

During colonial days, this salt marsh was a shallow bay bordered by Nell's Island. For thousands of years, Native Americans had fished here and gathered the plentiful oysters from the waters of the bay.

Blasting done in the late 1800s to improve boat navigation caused the bay to gradually fill with sediment, creating the present-day marsh. During migration, thousands of shore birds, herons, and waterfowl stop to rest and feed on the marsh's plentiful aquatic insects, fishes, and shellfish. In June, I watched a pair of nesting ospreys as well as snowy egrets, black ducks, and mute swans feeding in the management area. Great blue and green herons along with glossy ibis are also frequently seen here. Ducks, including the blue-winged teal and common merganser, are most often seen in spring and fall.

Opened in 1995, the Connecticut Audubon Coastal Center is built on the site of the former Milford Point Hotel, its mission: "To promote awareness of the Long Island Sound ecosystem and foster its preservation." The center features educational exhibits, a tide-pool touch tank, an inside observation area, equipped with spotting scopes, overlooking the Wheeler Wildlife Management Area, a salt-marsh laboratory, and program and meeting rooms. A covered observation tower offers panoramic views of the area. With the focus on environmental education, a variety of programs are offered for students, teachers, families, birders, and nature enthusiasts of all ages. It is the only education and research center in Connecticut dedicated exclusively to the study of the flora, fauna, and habitats of Long Island Sound.

Outside from the observation platform on the boardwalk, I watched piping plovers, semipalmated plovers, and sanderlings working the edge of the tide. I recall a visit with a friend some years ago in mid-May when we saw at least 16 species, including Canada and snow geese, buffleheads, American goldeneye ducks, and mallards as well as shore birds such as sanderlings, black-bellied plovers, and sandpipers.

The area of the sanctuary between the outer beach and the salt marsh is an excellent place to look for land birds, especially during migration.

From the boardwalk, it is just a short walk west along the shoreline to the observation deck at the entrance to the Milford Point Unit of the Stewart B. McKinney National Wildlife Refuge. When birding along the beach or walking to the National Wildlife Refuge, one must remember that the beach itself is privately owned and respect the rights of property owners. Walk below the high-tide line and do not use the private road that serves the homes along the beach.

This refuge was established to protect terns and plovers and is closed to birders during the nesting season from May to July. However, the observation deck is accessible year-round.

Listening to the calls of the gulls and nesting terns, and breathing the fresh salt air on a sunshine-filled day in June, made me indeed thankful for this unspoiled coastal area. The National Wildlife Refuge Observation deck, from April through September, is a likely place to observe great blue herons and snowy egrets as well as black-crowned night herons. Waterfowl, including black ducks and mallards, also feed and nest in the marsh.

Where: From I-95, exit 34, turn east onto U.S. 1. Go 0.2 mile to a light at Lansdale Avenue. Turn right on Lansdale and follow it to where it intersects with Milford Point Road. Turn right onto Milford Point Road. You will cross Naugatuck Avenue and pass tennis courts and Court Street. Stay on Milford Point Road to the junction of Seaview Avenue. Turn right and continue about 0.3 mile to the Connecticut Audubon Coastal Center at Milford Point. There is a sign at the entrance. The road forks right into the parking area. Do not take the road on the left, which is a private road.

Hours: The sanctuary is open year-round from dawn to dusk. The coastal center is open Tuesday to Saturday from 10:00 A.M. to 4:00 P.M., Sunday from noon to 4:00 P.M.

Admission: There is a small admission charge for those who are not members of the Connecticut Audubon Coastal Center.

Best time to visit: Any time of year is bound to be interesting at this sanctuary, but you will see the greatest number of species of birds during spring and fall migrations. Winter is a good time to see large numbers of ducks in the offshore waters.

Activities: Bird-watching, photography, nature study, and special programs, including youth programs, classes, lectures, and workshops related to environmental topics for beginning and experienced naturalists of all ages. Interpretive bird and nature walks and family canoe trips. The coastal center has parking for disabled people and an access ramp to the building. Not allowed are picnicking, swimming, and sunbathing.

Concessions: None.

Pets: No pets are allowed in the sanctuary. In addition, no dogs, even on a leash, are allowed on the beach (which is private) during nesting season, from April 1 to September 1.

For more information: Connecticut Audubon Coastal Center at Milford Point, 1 Milford Point Road, Milford, CT 06460. Call 203-878-7440.

Stewart B. McKinney National Wildlife Refuge, P.O. Box 1030, Westbrook, CT 06498. Call 860-399-2513.

Beardsley Zoo

In October 1998, I had an opportunity to visit Beardsley Zoo in Bridgeport for a behind-the-scenes tour of the park, led by assistant director Lisa Tryon. While I knew that exciting changes were in progress, improvements that reflect those that are taking place all over the country as zoos are transformed into centers of learning and conservation, I was totally unprepared for the changes that have occurred in this once old-fashioned zoo. Instead of animals in cages, we found the zoo's inhabitants housed in areas that replicated as nearly as possible their natural surroundings.

Beardsley Zoo dates back to the 1920s when the famous showman, P. T. Barnum paraded his circus animals through the park, a habit that prompted city officials to establish a zoo. Barnum donated some of his circus animals to the new zoo, which was simply a collection of caged animals placed in a park setting. Although the zoo grew over the years and the focus changed from entertainment to education and preservation of endangered species, administrators were often prevented from making major improvements by a lack of funds.

In May 1997, however, an important event occurred—the transfer of the zoo's ownership to the Connecticut Zoological Society, which used a state grant of more than $9 million to purchase the 29-acre zoological park surrounded by 188 acres of state-owned park lands.

Under the leadership of Gregg Dancho, the zoo's director since 1983, a master plan has been formulated for improving and expanding the zoo. Plans for the future include enlarging the zoo from 29 to 54 acres with triple the number of animals and restoring the original Victorian gardens. New exhibit areas will include a conservation area replicating the natural surroundings of North and South America and an Asian plateau. The Victorian Gardens will be part of a turn-of-the-century cultural area that will include animal sculptures and the zoo's historic greenhouse and rose trellises. The metal arbors that had fallen into disrepair are being replaced with new, cedar arbors. An educational center, built in Victorian style, is also planned, and a new restaurant opened in 1999.

What has already been accomplished makes Connecticut's only zoo an outstanding destination for family trips. Plexiglas walls have replaced the traditional iron bars on animal enclosures. Some residents such as the colorful peacocks strut among visitors. Most impressive is the New World Tropics Building, constructed several years ago out of the zoo's former dismal "monkey house." When you open the door, you find yourself in an Amazon rain forest. The exhibit includes a macaw nesting tree. Watching these colorful birds surrounded by lush tropical vegetation and exotic blooms is the next best thing to actually visiting a tropical rain forest. In addition, you have an up-close view of wildlife, an experience that would be hard to duplicate in the wild, including handsome black and gold howler monkeys and pale-headed saki monkeys. I especially recall two pigmy marmosets, the world's smallest primates, which are also part of the Rain Forest Exhibit. Another favorite of mine is the brilliantly colored scarlet ibis, a bird that inhabits the coastal areas of northern and eastern South America.

Most appreciated by staff is a state-of-the-art animal hospital, which allows them to provide better care for the animals.

Besides the new World Tropics Building, there are many other exhibits to see, including two Siberian tigers, wolves, pronghorn antelopes, bison, bald eagles, llamas, spectacled bears, which are native to South America, and otters, which are part of the "Backyard Pond" exhibit. There are also a "New England Farmyard" exhibit and the Carousel Building, which includes a seasonal operating carousel as well as a museum of restored antique carousel pieces.

Many of the animals such as the red wolves are part of the captive breeding program. Beardsley Zoo, in cooperation with zoos and aquariums throughout North America, is participating in this program that seeks to breed endangered species in the hope that the animals' natural habitats can be restored or made safe so the descendants of these animals now being bred in captivity can one day be released back into the wild. The red wolf, which was almost extinct, has been reintroduced back into its natural environment, raising hopes that the species can survive in the wild.

Where: From Route 8 south bound, take the White Plains Road exit, turn left onto East Main Street and follow the signs to the park entrance. From Route 8 north bound, take exit 5, and follow the signs for the zoo entrance.

Hours: Beardsley Zoo is open daily from 9:00 A.M. to 4:00 P.M. except Thanksgiving, Christmas, and New Year's Day. The New World Tropics Building is open from 10:30 A.M. to 3:30 P.M. The Carousel Museum is seasonal and is open from 10:30 A.M. to 4:00 P.M. The Zoo Gift Shop is open from 10:00 A.M. to 4:00 P.M.

Admission: There is an admission fee. Visitors over 61, those who are physically disabled, and children age 3 to 11 pay a reduced rate. Children under 3 are admitted free.

Best time to visit: Cooler weather and smaller crowds make spring or fall an ideal time to visit this zoo.

Activities: Seeing the live animal exhibits, touring the gardens, carousel (seasonal), restaurant, picnic area, and gift shop.

Pets: Not allowed.

For more information: Beardsley Zoo, 1875 Noble Avenue, Bridgeport, CT 06610. Call 203-394-6565. Website: www. beardsley.org.

3

Central Connecticut

The birds love an easy way,
and in the valleys of the rivers
they find a road already graded for them;
and they abound more in such places
throughout the season
than they do farther inland.

—JOHN BURROUGHS
Birds and Poets

Central Connecticut is a land of contrasts, ranging from large urban centers (Hartford and New Haven) to tranquil areas of fields, woods, and marshes bordering the Connecticut River and its tributaries.

The Connecticut River is a branch of the Atlantic Flyway. Great numbers of land birds, possibly as many as 200 species, follow the river valley during migration periods. At such times, woods that border the river and marshy areas provide food and resting places. In September, bird-watchers come to the Connecticut River to view a spectacular flight of hundreds and sometimes even thousands of hawks riding the thermal currents of air above the floodplain of the river as they migrate south.

Man, too, has always used the river as an avenue of transportation, from the time when Native Americans navigated the river in canoes and dugouts. Unfortunately, abuse of the river valley and degradation of the river's pure water paralleled industrial development in Connecticut. It is only in recent years that the impending loss of a great natural resource has been recognized and an effort made to clean up the river. Symbolic of people's interest in the river is the support being given to the effort to restore the Atlantic salmon to the Connecticut River and its tributaries. Although the project cannot yet be declared a success, the return of some salmon to their ancestral spawning grounds is proof of a vast improvement in water quality.

As you explore the river country, you will find trails to hike, rivers to fish or canoe, good areas for birding, views that are some of the most memorable in Connecticut, and a park where you can see tracks left in the mud by dinosaurs that roamed the Connecticut River Valley 200 million years ago.

Hill-Stead Museum

Hill-Stead Museum's colonial revival–style house, surrounded by gardens, farmland, and walking trails, transports you back to an earlier century. Located in Farmington, a town with numerous other interesting historic homes, Hill-Stead was designed as a retirement home for industrialist Alfred Atmore Pope and his wife, Ada Brooks Pope. Their architect daughter, Theodate, collaborated in designing the country home that was to be a showcase for the family's collection of French impressionist paintings as well as a working New England farm. Outside, the design called for a broad front lawn overlooking the valley below and, to the rear of the house, a rustic walking garden filled with woodland plants and a more formal sunken garden planted with perennials.

It is thought that the sunken garden was lost sometime in the early 1940s when it degenerated due to wartime labor shortages. When Hill-Stead was opened to the public as a museum in 1946, this important landscape feature was missing. In 1983, the Connecticut Valley Garden Club and the Garden Club of Hartford undertook the restoration of the sunken garden. Using an early 1900s design for the garden found in the archives of landscape architect Beatrix Farrand, the garden restorers completed their work in 1986, having reestablished 75 varieties of plants, primarily perennials. Visitors may obtain a garden plan and plant list for the sunken garden in the museum bookstore. In summer, when my friend Milly and I visited Hill-Stead, we found all the old favorites here, including summer phlox, delphinium, foxglove, and bellflower.

We also joined a guided tour of the house, which is furnished the way it was when the Pope family lived there. The impressive art collection contains many paintings and etchings by American artist James A. M. Whistler, a friend of the Popes. Most memorable of all, however, is the luminous light captured by Claude Monet in his seasonal haystack paintings.

The following spring I returned to Hill-Stead on a lovely day in April when the sun felt warm for the first time after an unusually cold, snowy winter. The red buds on the maple trees were beginning to swell, and in the woods the first delicate green leaves of wildflowers and shrubs transformed the drab winter landscape with their promise of new life. In the sunken garden, the soft pink blooms of a star magnolia signaled the arrival of spring, and I found glory-of-the-snow and daffodils just coming into bloom. A summerhouse in the center of the garden provided a quiet place to rest and enjoy the flowers.

From the parking area, I continued walking along the road past the old pump house, an orchard, a pond, and the farm meadows. Here, I was only dimly aware of the distant sound of traffic. I appreciated this view of the open fields and pond all the more for having just escaped from the heavy traffic on State 4, where commercial development has destroyed much of the surrounding countryside.

A map of the grounds and trails is available at the bookshop. One of several access points to the trails is just behind the parking area. From there I climbed a hill and entered a forest of tall hemlocks, where the only sounds were the calls of chickadees. A circular route takes you from the woods through fields and meadows and the old orchard back to the road near the pond. Special programs offered by the museum include nature walks to observe birdlife and wildflowers. The Hill-Stead trails also connect with the Metacomet Trail, part of the Connecticut Blue Trail system. The Metacomet Trail follows the traprock range running from the Hanging Hills of Meriden to the Massachusetts line for about 45 miles.

A visit to Hill-Stead offers an opportunity to combine viewing an impressive art collection, including originals by Claude Monet, Édouard Manet, and Edgar Degas, with touring a delightful garden and enjoying a pleasant nature walk or longer hike on the Metacomet Trail.

Where: The entrance is on Mountain Road off State 10 in Farmington.
Hours: The grounds are open from 7:00 A.M. to 5:00 P.M. year-round. The museum is open Tuesday through Sunday, 10:00 A.M. to 5:00 P.M., May through October; 11:00 A.M. to 4:00 P.M. the rest of the year. Call 860-677-4787 for a schedule. Hour-long guided house tours of the museum are offered every half hour, with the last tour beginning one hour before closing. Closed on major holidays.

Admission: Although there is no charge for admission to the grounds, a fee is charged for the house tour.

Best time to visit: May through August are the best months to see the gardens. Spring wildflowers are best in May. October is special for fall foliage walks.

Activities: Hiking, jogging, birding, cross-country skiing, painting, sketching, and museum tours. Picnicking and fishing are *not* allowed. A schedule of special programs includes a nature series and a Sunken Garden Poetry Festival in the summer.

Pets: Not allowed.

For more information: Hill-Stead Museum, 35 Mountain Road, Farmington, CT 06032. Call 860-677-4787.

Dinosaur State Park

The largest dinosaur track site in North America is in the Connecticut River Valley in the town of Rocky Hill. The site is preserved in Dinosaur State Park, a registered natural landmark. Here 500 of the early Jurassic tracks are on display, sheltered by the Exhibit Center's 122-foot geodesic dome.

The discovery of the tracks came in 1966 when bulldozer operator Ed McCarthy uncovered some unusual rocks during excavation work for a new state building. Action was then taken by the governor to preserve the site and establish a state park. The first excavation exposed nearly 1,500 tracks on a large area of bedrock. These tracks were eventually reburied for preservation. A second excavation in 1967 uncovered 500 more tracks, and those tracks are on display in the Exhibit Center. The tracks are of the type that had been named "Eubrontes" by a Massachusetts geologist in 1845.

When you look at the tracks preserved in the layers of sandstone, you are gazing at a record of life in the Connecticut River Valley 200 million years ago, when large carnivorous reptiles searched for prey along the edges of a large lake. Alone or in small groups, they waded in the shallow water searching for fish or small crocodilians. In the age of the dinosaurs, Connecticut had a semitropical climate. Some of the tracks you see were probably made as the dinosaurs crossed mudflats to rest in the upland forests of cycads, ginkgoes, tall stiff evergreens, and lush ferns.

The exact nature of the dinosaur that made the tracks that you will see in Dinosaur State Park remains a mystery. The tracks are three-toed impressions that vary in length from 10 to 16 inches. From the size of the tracks and the four-foot pace, it is known that the adult dinosaurs were about eight feet tall and 20 feet long. The skeletal remains that are the best match for the Eubrontes tracks are those of Dilophosaurus, a carnivorous dinosaur found in rocks of the same age in Arizona. A full-sized reconstruction of Dilophosaurus is on display in the Exhibit Center.

Discovery of Fossil Tracks and Bones of Dinosaurs

The Connecticut Valley has a long history of fossil-track discoveries, dating back to the beginning of the 19th century. Edward B. Hitchcock, who for many years was the president and professor of natural theology and geology at Amherst College, became interested in the tracks in 1835. From that date on, until his death in 1864, much of his time was devoted to the discovery and study of fossil tracks. His collection of tracks became so large that a museum was built in Amherst to house it. However, Hitchcock never knew that he had discovered dinosaur tracks. As long as he lived, he believed that he was looking at the tracks of ancient birds. Nevertheless, his work and collection were invaluable to future dinosaur hunters like Othniel Charles Marsh and Richard Swann Lull, who in 1922 became director of Yale University's Peabody Museum of Natural History.

Although many tracks have been discovered, few fossil bones have turned up in the Connecticut Valley. The best skeleton found in Connecticut was discovered in a stone quarry near Manchester. It was a nearly complete skeleton, six or seven feet in length, and was named by Marsh "Anchisaurus colurus." The discovery of another species of dinosaur in the same quarry came too late. Only the back part of the skeleton was present. The front part had already been built into the abutments of a bridge!

Recent improvements to the Exhibit Center include new lighting for better viewing, air-conditioning, new permanent exhibits, and improved access for visitors with disabilities. Housed under the geodesic dome are an 80-foot-long diorama depicting the setting in which the park's tracks were made and a 30-foot diorama of the Connecticut Valley during the late Triassic period.

Outside the Exhibit Center is a track-casting area where you may make a plaster cast of a real dinosaur track. Choose a good day for this project, because poor weather conditions will make casting difficult. You will need to bring supplies: a quarter cup of cooking oil, a five-gallon plastic bucket, 10 pounds of plaster of paris, cloth rags, and paper towels. The entire process takes about 30 to 45 minutes. Printed instructions are available at the park.

While dinosaur tracks are the big attraction, they are by no means the only reason to visit Dinosaur State Park. The discovery of the tracks led to the preservation of 70 acres of land with two miles of nature trails in an otherwise heavily developed area south of Hartford. Depending on the season, you can see spring wildflowers, some of the many birds that are attracted to the area, swamp-dwelling creatures such as frogs and salamanders, and insects. Most interesting is the boardwalk trail through the heart of a swamp. The boardwalk was constructed by the Youth Conservation Corps during the summer of 1976. Walking this trail while listening to the calls of frogs from the depths of the swamp, surrounded by tall shrubs and trees, one finds it easy to slip back in time to the period when the great dinosaurs roamed this area. A trail map and a checklist of birds seen at the park and in the vicinity are available at the trailhouse office. The list includes songbirds— such as thrushes, warblers, Baltimore and orchard orioles, and the scarlet tanager—as well as herons, the great horned owl, and the American woodcock. In all, 107 species have been recorded as seen within the boundaries of Dinosaur State Park.

The Meadow Nature Trail takes you past five small gardens, each of which has a different theme. The first is planted with garden flowers that are native to North America. In the past, these perennials were overlooked by growers in favor of species from Europe and Asia. Recently, the plant trade has begun to feature Connecticut's equally attractive native species, which are better suited to the hot, windy summers and cold winters. In another area, park staff are attempting to remove the most invasive species of European weeds, which settlers and their livestock brought with them from Europe and the Near East. It is widely feared that Connecticut's native wildflowers are being displaced by these hardy and aggressive plants. Two other gardens feature native meadow flowers, adapted to life in the sun, and meadow grasses. Contrary to popular belief, Connecticut was not entirely forested when the first settlers arrived from Europe. There were meadows in which native flowers and grasses flourished, supporting a great variety of insects, birds, and mammals.

Probably the favorite garden at the park is the Butterfly Garden, designed to attract butterflies for the enjoyment of visitors. Butterfly caterpillars need food plants such as the tall grasses, thistles, and milkweeds in the surrounding wildflower meadow. The adult butterflies need nectar plants like the flowers in the garden. It is hoped that these gardens will serve as a model and inspire homeowners to help these colorful insects survive. Butterflies are suffering a severe decline in Connecticut as land development destroys their natural habitat. As the display gardens' information sheet points out, "It would be a tragedy for us and our children to live in a world without butterflies."

Dinosaur State Park is open all year. In the winter, after a snowstorm, cross-country skiers follow the nature trails to look for animal tracks. Although many mammals are seldom seen, you can learn much from their tracks, which not only identify the animal but often tell you what that animal was doing. Common animal tracks you might see in the park are those of white-tailed deer, cottontail rabbits, opossums, gray squirrels, and deer mice. Children may be interested in making castings of the animal tracks they discover. An information sheet available at the park identifies the common tracks and gives instructions for making a plaster-of-paris cast.

Visitors come to Dinosaur State Park to learn about the past history of our planet, but the park also teaches us about life today, demonstrating ways we can help protect our wild-life and native plants so that the rich diversity of life we now enjoy will still be here for our children and future generations.

Where: The park is on West Street, one mile east of I-91 (exit 23) in Rocky Hill.

Hours: Open daily from 9:00 A.M. to 4:30 P.M. The track-casting area is open daily from 9:00 A.M. to 3:30 P.M. May 1 to October 31. The Exhibit Center is open Tuesday through Sunday from 9:00 A.M. to 4:30 P.M. year-round. Closed major holidays.

Admission: No fee is charged for admission to the park, but a fee is charged for admission to the Exhibit Center.

Best time to visit: The Exhibit Center may be crowded on summer weekends. Any other time is most enjoyable to visit this park.

Activities: Exhibit Center with dioramas, fossil tracks, and full-size reconstruction of a dinosaur. Walking along nature trails, viewing display gardens, making plaster casts of dinosaur tracks, museum shop, picnicking, cross-country skiing, and searching for animal tracks. (No food or bicycles are allowed on the trails.) Programs and trail walks are offered by park naturalists.

Concessions: None.

Pets: Pets are not allowed on trails or in Exhibit Center.

For more information: Dinosaur State Park, 400 West Street, Rocky Hill, CT 06067-3506. Call Infoline, 860-529-8423; staff, 860-529-5816.

Wadsworth Falls State Park

Wadsworth Falls State Park is best remembered for its pleas-ant wooded hiking trails and thundering 20-foot-high waterfall, which drops into a sunlit pool in the Coginchaug River. It is an easily accessible park with the entrance located in Middlefield on State 157. The park was given to the state in 1942 through the will of Colonel Clarence Wadsworth, a Middletown resident, who had devoted his life to civic endeavors and land preservation.

The wooded picnic area has tables and grills. Some tables overlook a small pond with a sandy beach, where you can swim in summer. Other facilities include rest rooms, changing rooms, and an outside water faucet.

The best time to hike the Main Trail to the falls is in the spring. Not only are the falls most impressive at this season, but also the mountain laurel is displaying its delicate pink blossoms. The trail begins just behind the picnic area and is marked with orange blazes. You cross a bridge over a small stream and, when the trail forks, follow the one to the right. Hiking through woods composed of maple, poplar, and birch, you pass a rare giant mountain laurel. Continuing along the trail, you notice the landscape changing, with more hickory, oak, and hemlock trees. The chattering of red squirrels is likely to be heard, and, depending on the time of day, you may catch a glimpse of a white-tailed deer. Hiking this trail one summer with a friend, I remember especially the feathery hemlocks along the slopes of the ravine. About three-quarters of a mile along, you reach a side trail to Little Falls on Wadsworth Brook. Big Falls is reached after a hike of a little more than one and a quarter miles from the start of the trail. Here the falling water cascades over volcanic traprock. The pool at the base of the falls is a favorite spot for trout fishermen.

Other short park trails that invite exploration are White Birch Trail, Deer Trail, Cedar Loop Trail, and Laurel Brook Trail.

Autumn, when the woods glow with the brilliant red leaves of the maples and the golden foliage of the hickories and birches, is also a good time to visit this park. I went there on a Sunday in late October and found myself in the company of many families who had come to hike or have a picnic amid the vibrant foliage on what turned out to be the last day of Indian-summer weather.

In winter, the parking area remains open for those who come to cross-country ski or snowshoe on designated trails or ice skate on the frozen pond. The Main Trail to the falls, Bridge Trail, White Birch Trail, and Cedar Loop Trail are all suitable for winter use.

Rangers are on duty during the summer season from Memorial Day through Labor Day but are not regularly available during the rest of the year. You can consult a carved map of the park's trails placed near the park entrance, and a trail map is also posted near the start of the Main Trail to the falls. However, if you are planning to hike here off-season, you may wish to obtain beforehand a trail map from the State Parks Division of the Connecticut Department of Environmental Protection.

Where: The park entrance is in Middlefield, on State 157, 1.6 miles southwest of the junction of State 66 and 157 in Middletown.

Hours: Open daily for day use from 8:00 A.M. to sunset as conditions permit.

Admission: A per-vehicle parking fee is in effect from Memorial Day weekend through Labor Day weekend.

Best time to visit: The park is busiest during summer months. Best time to hike is in spring and fall. In winter, after a fresh fall of snow, it is also a good place for an outing on cross-country skis or snowshoes.

Activities: Hiking, fishing, swimming, cross-country skiing, picnicking, and ice skating. No ranger-led activities offered.

Concessions: None.

Pets: Not allowed on the beach or in the brook area. Dogs on a leash are permitted on the hiking trails.

For more information: State Parks Division, Bureau of Outdoor Recreation, Connecticut Department of Environmental Protection, 79 Elm Street, Hartford, CT 06106-5127. Call 860-424-3200. Website: www.dep.state.ct.us.

Salmon River State Forest and Day Pond State Park

Five miles west of Colchester in eastern Connecticut, more than 6,000 acres of forested land have been preserved in Salmon River State Forest and adjacent Day Pond State Park. The acquisition of land for the state forest began in 1934 with the purchase of 286 acres on both sides of the Salmon River. Additional purchases have ensured the preservation of this unspoiled natural area of the Salmon River Valley. A favorite haunt of trout fishermen and whitewater-canoeing enthusiasts, the river flows swiftly, swirling around boulders. Stands of hemlock line the riverbank, where the silence is broken by the murmuring of flowing water.

I first saw the Salmon River from the Comstock Covered Bridge, located just off State 16 in East Hampton. The Comstock Bridge, one of the few covered bridges left in Connecticut, was donated to the state by the towns of East Hampton and Colchester and restored by the Civilian Conservation Corps in 1936. The roadside area by the bridge has picnic tables. It's a prime spot to stop for a picnic or to fish, and you can walk across the bridge, which is limited to foot travel and connects the two parts of the forest.

The entrance to Salmon River State Forest is on the right, off State 16, just east of the covered bridge. On this warm day in late May, the area, which has a recreation field and picnic site, was uncrowded. White dogwoods were in bloom, and the sweet fragrance of pine filled the air as I walked toward the river through a stand of tall white pines. Along the riverbank are picnic tables and easy access points for fishing. I envied two girls who had placed their lounge chairs in the river, a delightful way to get some sun and keep cool at the same time.

The Salmon River, which is formed in Hebron by the confluence of several brooks, flows in a southwesterly direction to the Connecticut River at Haddam Neck. As a tributary of the Connecticut River, the Salmon is playing an important role in the effort to restore Atlantic salmon to the Connecticut River system. Each spring, all along the Connecticut River from its source near the Canadian border to where it empties into the sea near Old Lyme, Connecticut, millions of fry and young salmon, seven to nine inches long, are released into the river and its tributaries. At Salmon River State Forest, two cement stream-fed "imprint" ponds hold young salmon from hatcheries each spring before they are released to depart on their long journey to the ocean. After two years, the salmon find their way back as adults by recognizing the odor of the water in which they were held. To provide maximum protection for the young Atlantic salmon, which are generally under nine inches in length, trout taken from the Salmon River must be at least nine inches long, and any salmon caught must be released immediately.

The effort to restore the salmon to their ancestral home has its disappointments. It doesn't take much effort to imagine the hazards the salmon encounter on a journey that takes them to their feeding grounds off the coast of Greenland and back to New England; but salmon are returning, and for those who have seen one, it is a thrilling experience. The fact that salmon can now live in the Connecticut River is a great accomplishment in itself. As recently as the mid-1950s, much of the river was still badly polluted. For many, the return of the salmon is a symbol of hope that we can reverse the damage that has been done to our fragile planet. Perhaps most encouraging is the fact that the first known truly wild salmon hatched at the mouth of the Salmon River in the spring of 1992. These native salmon returned to their river of origin in 1996.

The entrance to Day Pond State Park is off State 149, which crosses State 16 a short distance east of the state-forest entrance. The pond, which now attracts visitors with its sandy beach, was constructed by a pioneering family by the name of Day. The pond water was used to turn a large waterwheel that powered the family's sawmill. Surrounding the park are inviting woodlands where oak, maple, beech, tulip, silver birch, hickory, and hemlock trees predominate. Picnic sites with tables and grills are scattered around the pond. A large picnic shelter, accessible to visitors who are disabled, is located near the entrance overlooking the pond. It is equipped with tables and benches and two large fieldstone fireplaces for cookouts.

Spring is a good time to visit this park. On a day in late May, the woods were bright with the white blossoms of dogwood and the delicate pink blooms of wild azaleas. June, when the mountain laurel flowers, should be an equally good time. Wildflowers and ferns also abound. While I ate lunch at a site overlooking the pond, from somewhere hidden in the woods came the sound of classical music, a fitting accompaniment to the songs of birds, the whisper of a breeze through the trees, and the laughter of children down on the beach.

For hiking, access to a trail that loops four miles through the park and Salmon River State Forest is on the right, past the beach, just before the dam. This blue-blazed trail through mainly deciduous woods takes you to the crest of a hill from which you can view the Salmon River Valley.

Where: The covered bridge is on Comstock Bridge Road, off State 16 in East Hampton. The entrance to Salmon River State Forest is on the opposite side of State 16, just east of the bridge. Day Pond State Park is 5.5 miles west of Colchester off State 149.

Hours: Salmon River State Forest and Day Pond State Park are open from 8:00 A.M. to sunset, year-round, as conditions permit.

Admission: No charge at Salmon River State Forest. At Day Pond State Park, there is a charge for parking on weekends and holidays from Memorial Day through Labor Day.

Best time to visit: Spring to see flowering shrubs, wildflowers, and ferns. Fall for hiking amid glowing foliage, although it is best to visit before the start of hunting season, because hunting is allowed in Salmon River State Forest. Summer for swimming and picnics in Day Pond State Park. Winter for cross-country skiing in Salmon River State Forest.

Activities: Salmon River State Forest—hiking, picnicking, fishing, hunting, and cross-country skiing. Picnic tables are accessible to visitors with disabilities.

Day Pond State Park—swimming, hiking, nature trail, picnicking, picnic shelter, horseback riding, and fishing. (The pond is stocked with trout.) Picnicking, picnic shelter, horseback riding, and fishing are all accessible to visitors with disabilities.

Concessions: None.

Pets: No pets are allowed on the beach in Day Pond State Park. Pets on a leash are allowed on hiking trails.

For more information: State Parks Division, Bureau of Outdoor Recreation, Connecticut Department of Environmental

Protection, 79 Elm Street, Hartford, CT 06106-5127. Call 860-424-3200. Website: www.dep.state.ct.us.

Devil's Hopyard State Park

Devil's Hopyard State Park in East Haddam, where the Eight Mile River flows through a wild and scenic ravine, became Connecticut's 21st state park in 1919. Steep hillsides forested with hemlocks line the river and attract both migrant and nesting warblers, vireos, and thrushes. However, most of the 100,000 visitors who come to the park each year want to see the park's principal feature, Chapman Falls, which drop more than 60 feet over a series of steps in a Scotland schist stone formation. The falls were named after John Chapman, who once operated the gristmill and sawmill at this location, known as "Beebe's Mills" after the original owner. The gristmill closed in 1854, but the sawmill continued in operation until the mid-1890s.

On a warm summer weekday I found the park uncrowded. In fact, my friend Carolyn and I had one of the spacious, cool picnic sites along the river all to ourselves. After our lunch, we followed the trail to the top of Chapman Falls, where we looked down on the water cascading in a series of falls over ledges into quiet pools scoured out in the rock bed of the river. Along the sides of the gorge are large potholes, some of the finest examples of pothole stone formation in New England. Potholes are formed when a stone from upstream becomes trapped in an eddy and is spun around and around until it wears a cylindrical depression in the rock.

To superstitious early settlers, the potholes were a great mystery. Their attempt to explain how the potholes came to be there is the source of one of the many stories of how the park got its name. According to this legend, the devil, passing by the falls, happened to get his tail wet, which made him hopping mad, mad enough to burn holes in the stone with his hooves as he bounded away!

Cross a covered bridge in the pic-nic area, and you are at the start of the Devil's Oven Trail, which climbs 150 feet over a series of ledges to a scenic overlook. Other trails lead to a trapper's sod hut, Baby Falls, and the Devil's Tombstone.

During May and June, Devil's Hopyard State Park is one of the best areas in Connecticut to see migrant and nesting birds. Near the beginning of the path that leads to the picnic area, you will notice some mag-nificent white oaks, which are favorite nesting sites for blue-gray gnatcatchers. You can easily identify this tiny blue-gray bird with its white belly, long, twitching tail, and wheezy but melodious warble. Its nest, fashioned of plant down and fibers held together with spiderwebs, holds four or five bluish eggs spotted with reddish brown. Other birds to look for in this area are redstarts, ovenbirds, and chestnut-sided, blue-winged, and black-and-white warblers.

In the thickets of mountain laurel that grow on the hill-sides, you may catch a glimpse of the hooded warbler. The black hood and yellow face make the male easy to identify. In the hemlocks along the river near the picnic area, you may see the Acadian flycatcher, a rare species in Connecticut, which nests in this park. This shy bird of the deep forests is recog-nized by its greenish gray back, buff-colored wing bars, light eye rings, and sides washed with yellow.

Scarlet tanagers, rose-breasted grosbeaks, wood pewees, wood thrushes, veeries, and eastern bluebirds also nest in this park. Great-horned, barred, and screech owls nest in the area, as well as red-tailed and red-shouldered hawks. In early May, the river valley is on the flyway for migrating warblers, while in late August large flocks of nighthawks may be observed following this same route. For the migrating nighthawks, it is a long journey from Connecticut to South America, where they spend the winter.

If you camp in this park and get up very early in the morning, you'll have the best chance of seeing birds. Devil's Hopyard State Park has 21 wooded sites located near Chapman Falls. For those who like old-fashioned camping, it's a good place to come to enjoy bird-watching, hiking, or fishing. Each site has a table and a fireplace. The well and hand pump bring back memories of an earlier time. The sanitary facilities are of the primitive kind, too. In case of inclement weather, there is a shelter in the picnic area. This park is best for short-term camping in spring or fall. In summer, the park may be crowded, and the no-swimming regulation leaves campers without any way to cool off on a hot day.

The Eight Mile River provides good fishing for brook trout. In addition, American and lamprey eels travel to the pool at the bottom of the falls each spring.

Where: Three miles north of the intersection of State 82 and 156.

Hours: Open daily for day use from 8:00 A.M. to sunset. The campground is open from mid-April to September 30. However, check with the State Parks Division office if you plan to camp before Memorial Day weekend or after Labor Day.

Admission: No fee for day use. There is a daily campsite fee for camping.

Best time to visit: Spring and fall when the park is uncrowded are the best times to visit.

Activities: Bird-watching, hiking, camping, stream fishing, and picnicking. No ranger-led activities are offered.

Concessions: None.

Pets: Not allowed in the campground or near the river or falls. Pets on a leash are allowed on wooded hiking trails.

For more information: Devil's Hopyard State Park, 366 Hopyard Road, East Haddam, CT 06423. Call 860-873-8566.

Gillette Castle State Park

Gillette Castle State Park in Hadlyme is outstanding not only for its impressive medieval-style fortress, the former home of the celebrated actor and playwright William Gillette, but also

Gillette Castle

for the magnificent view it affords of the Connecticut River. Although the river has suffered three centuries of abuse by man, including pollution of its waters and uncontrolled development along its banks, the Lower Connecticut River Valley between East Haddam and Old Saybrook remains remarkably unspoiled. A sandbar at the mouth of the river has kept out deep-draft vessels and saved the river from the intensive development common to other major rivers. In recent years, federal, state, and local governments have spent more than $600 million in an attempt to clean up the Connecticut River and preserve its natural resources, including fish and wildlife. From Hartford south, the Connecticut becomes a tidal river.

Downstream from Gillette Castle, near the mouth of the river in Old Lyme, ospreys nest on Great Island. The island has tidal channels that from November to April are frequented by many species of ducks, including buffleheads, greater scaup, and American goldeneyes. In addition, the Lower Connecticut River Valley is the winter home of some 20 bald eagles. David and Deborah Ritchie report in their guide, *Connecticut Off the Beaten Path*, that in late winter or early spring, it is sometimes possible to stand on the main terrace of Gillette Castle and watch eagles soar over the river.

William Gillette and His Castle

Born July 24, 1853, William Gillette, noted actor and playwright, is best known for his portrayal of Sherlock Holmes. A Connecticut native, born and educated in Hartford, Gillette, at the height of his career in 1913, decided to build the home he had been dreaming of for years. Gillette was a man who loved nature in all its forms. He especially loved the Connecticut River and spent much of his free time cruising the river on his houseboat, the *Aunt Polly*. He had almost decided to build his home near Greenport, Long Island, when, by chance, he anchored his boat near the east-bank slip of the Chester-Hadlyme ferry. Impressed by the rugged hill towering above the river, he decided to climb it the next morning. He was in the area of a series of hills along the river known as the Seven Sisters. When he reached the summit of the southernmost hill, he was so impressed by the splendid view of the river far below, bordered by forested hills and ridges of rock, that he immediately set about purchasing 122 acres of land adjacent to the ferry landing.

Gillette built his home on the summit of this hill and named it Seventh Sister. Constructed of native granite with southern white oak used in the interior, the castle took five years to complete and required the services of 22 skilled masons. With great inventive ability and a total disregard for conventional ways, Gillette designed everything for the interior as well as for the grounds of his home. Of the 47 doors within the castle, no two are exactly the same, and each has a handsome, intricately carved wooden latch. His creative ability is also evident in the built-in couches, a movable table on tracks, and the light switches of carved wood.

Gillette lived to be nearly 84 years old. Following his death in 1937, his estate was acquired by the State Park and Forest Commission. It had been William Gillette's wish that Seventh Sister and its extensive grounds be preserved for the benefit of others who would appreciate its great natural beauty as well as the creative genius that inspired the building of the castle. Today, the uniqueness of the castle draws over 100,000 visitors to tour it annually, hike the trails, and take in the sweeping views that were once a cherished part of William Gillette's life.

At the close of the summer season in September 1998, the castle was closed to visitors for renovations. Repairs are being made to the roof and to the parapet of the castle as well as to the 12-foot-high stone masonry walls that run along the park roads. Check with the park for the reopening date, which is expected to be Memorial Day, the start of the summer season in the year 2000. The park grounds are remaining open throughout the reconstruction.

Chester-Hadlyme Ferry

Despite the popularity of Gillette Castle State Park, it is still quite possible to find times to visit when the park is uncrowded. I found such a time on a weekday in late September when the first hint of autumn was just beginning to give color to the Connecticut hills. I stood on the main terrace for a long time enjoying the breathtaking view and the splendor of the terrace garden, still in bloom. Herring gulls circled over the river, and I watched a hawk riding the thermal currents. Far below, the ferryboat *Seldon III* was making its way back and forth across the Connecticut River. The Chester-Hadlyme Ferry has been in continuous operation since 1769. It is one of two historic ferries owned and operated by the Connecticut Department of Transportation. (The other is the Glastonbury–Rocky Hill Ferry, which, in operation since 1655, is the oldest continuously operating ferry in the United States.) *The Seldon III*, which departs from the ferry landing on State 148 in Chester from April 1 to December 19, including holidays except Thanksgiving, can carry eight cars. Taking the ferry is a nice way to approach Gillette Castle.

Hiking Trails and Narrow-Gauge Railroad

Some of the trails in the park follow Gillette's own walking paths, which he constructed with steps and stone-arch bridges. Trail maps are available. Gillette, who was a railroad buff, also built on his property a three-mile-long narrow-gauge railroad. In December 1997, Lake Compounce Amusement Park in Bristol gave back to the state of Connecticut Gillette's custom-made train, making it possible for the 71-year-old electric train to once again transport visitors along the old railroad bed that winds its way through the woods and a rocky glen.

I followed one of the trails around a small lily-covered pond. The only sound was that of frogs diving beneath the lily pads as I approached. Near the water's edge, I watched a monarch butterfly sipping nectar in a clump of goldenrod.

Picnic Areas

Gillette Castle State Park is a fine place to go for a picnic. The main picnic area is wooded with oaks and hemlocks, which provide shade on a hot summer's day. However, on this cool fall day, I sought out a sunny table. While I ate lunch, I watched several gray squirrels feeding on the abundant crop of acorns. Nearer the castle, tables on a covered pavilion, as well as other choice picnic sites, offer a sweeping view of the river valley.

Canoeing and River Cruises

The Lower Connecticut River is a favorite area for boating, especially sailing and canoeing. By advance reservation only, canoes may be rented near the ferry slip below Gillette Castle State Park. There is a minimum of four canoes for daily rentals and two canoes for overnight rentals.

For those who choose to explore the river by canoe, several state parks along the river provide shore access for picnicking, hiking, or camping. Selden Neck State Park, one and a half miles downstream on the left bank, covers 528 acres and is an undeveloped park with riverside campsites available from May

1 through September 30. Accessible only by water, the park has hiking trails with drinking water, fireplaces, and sanitary facilities for campers.

At the mouth of the Connecticut River, a water trail for kayakers and canoeists has been established in the Great Island marsh area with the help of a grant from Connecticut's "Preserve the Sound" license plate fund. It is a network of canoe and kayak-accessible trails through creeks and tidal marshes of the Connecticut River, Black Hall River, and the Lieutenant River, as well as the creeks in the area of Great Island. The starting point is the state-owned boat ramp at the end of Smith's Neck Road in Old Lyme. An informational brochure and map is available from state tourist information centers, local town halls, libraries, sporting goods stores, and nature organizations.

North of Gillette Castle State Park, about six miles south of Middletown on the east bank, Hurd State Park has good facilities for canoe camping, including water, tables, and a shelter. Two and a half miles below Hurd State Park, Haddam Island, and Haddam Meadows State Park on the west bank are good places for boaters to stop for a picnic, but neither has camping facilities.

Although in its lower reaches the Connecticut River has retained much of its natural beauty, it is by no means free of development. In Haddam Neck, the Connecticut Yankee Atomic Power Company's nuclear generating station rises from the east bank. Also, the river has commercial traffic. If you decide to canoe the Connecticut River, you will have to watch out for tankers that make the journey from Hartford to Long Island Sound. Large yachts also travel the river, and their wakes can easily swamp a canoe or other small boat.

For those who prefer to let someone else do the navigating on this big river, Camelot Cruises offers a marvelous all-day cruise from Marine Park in Haddam, Connecticut, to Sag

Harbor or Greenport on Long Island. You will learn about the river's history along the way. The cruise ship departs every day at 9:00 A.M. from June through Labor Day. Fall foliage lunch cruises are also offered from late September through early November.

Being on a boat in the river offers a great vantage point from which to observe birds. The whole Connecticut River Valley from the Connecticut Lakes in northern New Hampshire to Long Island Sound is a branch of the Atlantic Flyway. During spring and fall migrations, great numbers of land birds follow the river. In September, the Connecticut River is a good place to observe migrating hawks. While I saw only a lone hawk, hundreds and even thousands of hawks are sometimes seen during the peak days of the migration.

The Future of the Lower Connecticut River

For nearly three decades, those who cherish the Connecticut River have been laboring to ensure its preservation for future generations. In 1966, then-Senator Abraham Ribicoff introduced legislation authorizing a comprehensive study of the river valley. The resulting report recommended that the federal government take action to preserve three of the most valuable sections of the river, including the Lower Connecticut River Valley. A subsequent bill drafted by Ribicoff and unanimously approved by the U.S. Senate created a Connecticut Historic Riverway in the area between East Haddam and Old Saybrook known as the "Gateway Area." However, the Historic Riverway National Park that Ribicoff envisioned never materialized. The proposal to create a national park along the river was defeated by residents in the towns bordering the river who feared loss of local control over land use. They also objected to additional land being set aside for public recreation. Fortunately, the efforts to preserve the river didn't stop with the defeat of this bill. The Silvio Conte National Fish and Wildlife Act of 1991 authorized the U.S. Fish and Wildlife Service to consider the Connecticut River basin as a refuge. In the fall of 1993, the federal agency began informational hearings in the Lower Connecticut River Valley, explaining the proposal and gathering input from residents. The refuge proposal emphasizes cooperation with local groups as well as private owners. So far the proposal has received a generally favorable response. Residents who live near the river are quite aware of the abuse the river has suffered over the years and of the need for some kind of public control over land use. In 1995, Federal Conservation officials proposed a $135 million plan to create a national fish and wildlife refuge to protect invaluable plant and animal habitats in the Connecticut River Valley over the next 15 years. In 1998, the Connecticut River was designated one of the 10 "American Heritage Rivers" by President Clinton. It is hoped that this Gateway Area of the Connecticut River, site of Gillette Castle and winter home to bald eagles, an area that provides urgently needed feeding and resting areas for migrating birds, can enter the 21st century as part of the National Wildlife Refuge system.

Fishing

In colonial times, the Connecticut River had an abundant population of many species of fish. Salmon, weighing up to 30 pounds, and thousands of barrels of shad were harvested from the river. The construction of dams, which blocked access to the best spawning grounds, along with pollution of the water, changed all that. The salmon disappeared, and the shad run was reduced to a tiny fraction of its original numbers. In recent years, efforts to bring back the salmon through the construction of fish ladders and protection of spawning grounds has benefited the shad as well as the salmon. In addition, efforts have been made to clean up the river through the construction of sewage treatment plants. Salmon are once again returning to their ancient spawning grounds, and shad are returning to the Connecticut River in record numbers. The shad run usually begins in late April and ends by the middle of June. Largemouth bass are found in most sections of the river. In addition, panfish such as yellow perch and bluegill are abundant. A fishing license is required for resident as well as nonresident fishermen.

Although fish populations are increasing, further reduction of pollution is needed before a refreshing swim can be an enjoyable part of a visit to this historic river.

Where: Four miles south of East Haddam on State 82.
Hours: Open daily for day use from 8:00 A.M. to sunset. When it reopens, the castle will be open daily for tours from Memorial Day through Columbus Day from 10:00 A.M. to 5:00 P.M. It is open weekends only, 10:00 A.M. to 4:00 P.M., after Columbus Day through the fourth weekend after Thanksgiving. It has become a holiday tradition for many to visit the castle in December when the rooms are decorated for the holidays.
Admission: No fee for use of the park. An admission fee is charged to tour the castle.
Best time to visit: The park may be crowded during weekends

in summer and especially during fall foliage season. Otherwise, any time is a good time to visit this park.

Activities: Hiking, picnicking, touring the castle, fishing, canoeing, scenic overlook of the Connecticut River Valley, horse-drawn carriage rides, and narrow-gauge railroad rides.
Concessions: There is a gift and souvenir shop. From Memorial Day weekend through Labor Day weekend, there is a food concession and rental canoes are available by advance reservation only. For information on outfitting and transportation, contact North American Canoe Tours, Inc., 65 Black Point Road, Niantic, CT 06357. Call 860-739-0791.
Pets: Pets on a leash are allowed in the park. Pets are not permitted inside the castle.
For more information: Gillette Castle State Park, 67 River Road, Hadlyme, CT 06439. Call 860-526-2336.

Camelot Cruises, Inc., 1 Marine Park, Haddam, CT 06438. Call 860-345-8591.

Hammonasset Beach State Park

In a state where much of the shoreline is privately owned, Hammonasset State Park in Madison, with its two miles of sandy beach on Long Island Sound, is crowded and often noisy in summer; but in spring and fall, the beach, fields, extensive marshes bordering the Hammonasset River, cedar woods, and thicket hedges belong to the bird-watcher, beachcomber, kite-flier, and refugee from the city who, tired of urban living, come to walk a deserted beach where the only sounds are the lap of gentle waves along the shore and the cry of seagulls overhead, a place where they can escape the smog and breathe fresh salt air.

I must confess that until I revisited this state park in 1994, I didn't associate such a place with Connecticut. When I think about favorite unspoiled mainland beaches in New England, places like Reid State Park in Maine come to mind, but on a beautiful spring day in May, I discovered that Hammonasset was not the park I remembered. Much has been done to restore the natural beauty of this coastal park. Plantings of beach grass and native shrubs have helped to stabilize the dunes and prevent further erosion. From the first parking area, a path leads between the dunes out to West Beach. It is important to obey the regulations and stay off the dunes. Beach plants are fragile and easily destroyed. Plantings of pine trees in the area between the beach and the parking lot provide shade for picnic tables overlooking the dunes and ocean. There are paths and a boardwalk along the beach, but nature lovers and beachcombers will probably prefer walking on the hard sand at the edge of the tide, where the retreating waves leave behind their treasure of seashells and shining pebbles.

Even the camping area, which I remembered as a large field with sites crowded together, has been vastly improved with the planting of trees and shrubs and the reduction in the number of campsites from more than 900 to 558.

From West Beach, it is a short walk to the large enclosed pavilion where a food concession operates during the summer months. There's a large deck with picnic tables overlooking the beach and sound.

From West Beach, I drove past East Beach to the parking area for Meig's Point, one of the best areas to see shore and water birds as well as migrating land birds in Connecticut. From the parking area, you can follow a loop road that borders the edge of a vast tidal marsh on the Hammonasset River. At the far end of this loop, you will find the beginning of the nature trail to Willard's Island, actually a woodland surrounded by tidal marsh, which provides a haven for migrating forest songbirds. In spring and fall, sparrows, warblers, thrushes, mockingbirds, and woodpeckers use the island as a stop-off point.

However, on this day I was looking for shorebirds, and scanning the salt marsh from the loop road turned out to be an exciting adventure. Out in the marsh were five medium-sized birds, which at a distance looked black. Through field glasses, I could see their bronzy chestnut feathers and long decurved bills. With the help of a couple of other bird-watchers and Peterson's *Field Guide to the Birds*, it was agreed that this small flock had to be eastern glossy ibis, a sighting that was later confirmed by the Audubon Shop in Madison, which maintains a record of current bird sightings in the area. The breeding range of this bird extends around the world. It is found in Spain, Greece, China, and Australia; but in the United States, until recently, the glossy ibis was found primarily in the marshes of Lake Okeechobee and along the Gulf Coast in Florida. In his book *North with the Spring*, Edwin Way Teale describes watching flocks of glossy ibis returning at sunset to their roost among the low willows on King's Bar in Lake Okeechobee. Some birds do wander north, and sightings in Connecticut are not as rare as they once were, yet watching these southern birds feeding in a Connecticut marsh was the highlight of the day for me.

Several killdeer were feeding in the marsh as well as in a shallow pool of rainwater in the field opposite the marsh. The dark double breastband makes these birds easy to identify. This hardy bird is found in meadows and along the borders of pasture ponds as often as it is found near salt water. Beetles, grasshoppers, and other insects are the killdeer's favorite foods. Its nest, which consists of a shallow depression in the ground lined with grass, is found in barren, open areas such as plowed fields or gravel bars. When they are disturbed, a loud "kill-dee" is their cry of alarm.

Later, two snowy egrets were sighted. This handsome bird was previously killed in great numbers to provide feathers for the millinery trade. By the beginning of the 20th century, it had become rare and in danger of disappearing entirely from its favorite haunts—shallow ponds and quiet saltwater lagoons. Thanks to the passage of laws to protect the species and efforts to protect its breeding colonies, the species recovered, and today thousands of snowy egrets grace the shallow waters of our marshes and ponds.

This was also the right time to see the ospreys nesting on the platform that had been erected for them toward the northern end of the marsh. The food of the osprey consists entirely of fish. For successful fishing, the osprey needs clear water and fish that swim or feed near the surface. In salt water, the common prey are mullet, menhaden, and herring. Since the ban on the use of DDT, the osprey population has been increasing in Connecticut. The provision of platforms in suitable areas has increased the availability of nesting sites for the osprey, a bird that almost disappeared in Connecticut because of the unwarranted use of a dangerous pesticide.

I went down to the outer beach at Meig's Point to eat lunch, sheltered from the wind by a huge boulder. Climbing the trail up this rocky point of land brings you to a good vantage point to look for seabirds. Today, there were only a few ducks, but Dr. Noble Proctor, a leading authority on Connecticut birds, reports that loons, ducks, flocks of double-crested cormorants in spring and fall, and red-necked grebes in February have been seen from this location.

While I ate, herring gulls circled overhead, hoping for a snack. Herring and great black-backed gulls are both present at Hammonasset Beach. The gulls have become the English sparrows of the seabird world, disliked for their aggressive behavior toward other seabirds. Today, they are as common in the parking lots of shopping malls as they are on ocean beaches;

yet, with their plaintive cry and graceful flight, the gulls circling just above the waves have always symbolized for me the beauty of the New England coast. Once again, on that spring day at Meig's Point, I welcomed the presence of the gulls.

Where: One mile south of exit 62 off I-95 in Madison.
Hours: Open daily for day use from 8:00 A.M. to sunset, year-round, as conditions permit. Campground is open from the weekend before Memorial Day weekend until November 1. Check with the park office first if you are planning to camp before Memorial Day weekend or after Labor Day weekend.
Admission: Daily parking fee during the summer months. In addition, there is a charge on weekends only from mid-April through the weekend prior to Memorial Day weekend and again from Labor Day through the last weekend in September. Campers pay a nightly fee per campsite.
Best time to visit: Spring and fall to see waterfowl and land birds. The park is crowded in summer.
Activities: Swimming, scuba diving, camping, fishing, bird-watching, picnicking, hiking, and boating. During the summer season, a nature center is open, and there are interpretive programs. Don't miss out on the observation platform at Meig's Point.

There is excellent fishing from the stone jetty constructed during the winter of 1978–79. You can fish for saltwater species such as flounder and bass. A launching site is provided for fishermen who bring their own boats.

The campground has 558 mostly open sites. Facilities include flush toilets, showers, and a dumping station. Individual fireplaces are not provided.

Activities accessible to visitors who are disabled include camping, picnicking, and picnic shelters.
Concessions: A food concession is operated during the summer months.

Pets: Not allowed.

For more information: Hammonasset Beach State Park, Box 271, Madison, CT 06443. Call campground office, 203-245-1817; park office, 203-245-2785.

The Audubon Shop, 871 Boston Post Road, Madison, CT 06443. Call 203-245-9056 for information on birds seen and spring and fall bird walks at Hammonasset Beach State Park.

4

Northeastern Connecticut

*. . . for those who find their pleasure
out-of-doors, . . . all the years of existence
represent a long love affair with the earth. . . ."*

—Edwin Way Teale
A Naturalist Buys an Old Farm

Connecticut's "Quiet Corner" is sparsely populated, characterized by dense forests of white pine and northern hardwoods and many lakes and ponds, a rolling plateau of land divided by three rivers—the Natchaug, the Willimantic, and the Quinebaug. State forests and parks have helped to preserve much of the region's forestland along with some of the most scenic lakes and ponds. My favorite park in this area is Bigelow Hollow State Park, where the lakes and forests remind me of those in Maine and Ontario.

It is this region of Connecticut that author and naturalist Edwin Way Teale and his wife, Nellie, chose for their retirement home. Today, you can visit their farm, Trail Wood, now a sanctuary of the Connecticut Audubon Society.

"For those who find their pleasure out-of-doors," Connecticut's northeast corner will provide a lifetime of memories of quiet walks and scenic places, where the possibility of seeing wildlife turns even an afternoon stroll into an exciting adventure.

Bigelow Hollow State Park

One of my favorite places in northeastern Connecticut is a state park that reminds me of the lakes and forests of Maine and Ontario. There is a reason for this feeling of being in the north country, for Bigelow Hollow State Park in Union is an example of a Canadian Zone pocket of forest that attracts some species of birds that usually nest far to the north. Magnolia, Nashville, black-throated blue, and blackburnian warblers nest in the spruce and pine woods. In the thick growth of mountain laurel that covers the hillsides, the solitary vireo builds its nest. Here, too, on the rocky slopes, the winter wren, a bird more likely to be found breeding in northern Ontario, will nest, and its song, a succession of warbles and trills, may be heard on a spring bird walk.

If you want to see even more species of warblers, plan to visit this park in early May. In Connecticut, the height of the warbler migration occurs during the first two weeks of May, and the route of nearly all these wood warblers takes them through Bigelow Hollow State Park.

I first discovered this park several years ago in late May on a bird-watching trip to eastern Connecticut. The drive took me north on State 198 through the Natchaug River Valley, where lilacs were in bloom and a new growth of foliage and spring wildflowers brightened the woods and fields. When I turned north on State 171, I entered another world of sunlit evergreen forests. I began to see birds even before I reached the park. A bright flash of orange-and-black wings was a Baltimore oriole. A gray bird, the size of a robin, with large white patches on its wings and tail, was also easy to recognize as an eastern mockingbird; and I had a good look at a pair of purple finches when I slowed down for two birds in the middle of the road!

At the junction with State 197, I continued west. A right turn, which is easily missed, takes you into the 513-acre park, which contains two lakes. Stopping first at the lower lake, known as Bigelow Pond, where there is a nice picnic area, I walked down to the water's edge and scanned the surface of the pond and marshy areas along the shore. While I failed to spot any activity, I knew that wood ducks and occasionally hooded mergansers nest in this area. Both have benefited from the nesting-box program. The pond and the upper lake (Mashapaug Lake) also attract other waterfowl, including mallards, black ducks, ring-necked ducks, and great blue and green herons. During migration periods, birders may even see common loons or pied-billed grebes.

Leaving the first parking area, I drove to the end of the park road, where there is a second parking area and a gravel boat-launching ramp on the shore of Mashapaug Lake. This upper lake is a jewel with clear water, deep blue in the center where it mirrors the sky, and shades of emerald green in the coves, where tall spruces and hemlocks grow to the water's edge. Inviting rocky ledges and small islands add to the feeling that you are far to the north. To the left of the boat ramp, a trail leads through the woods to a picnic area on a forested point overlooking the lake. Birds were everywhere, but difficult to see as they alighted in the very tops of tall trees. Listening to a medley of spring birdsong, I ate my lunch and watched a small flock of white-throated sparrows feeding nearby. The nest of this sparrow, made of grass and moss, is often found along the brushy edges of a spruce forest. In it, the female lays four or five spotted greenish eggs. The clear, pensive notes of the white-throat's song are synonymous with the arrival of spring in the northern forests.

According to Dr. Noble Proctor, an authority on Connecticut's birds, both ruby-crowned and golden-crowned kinglets, birds that usually nest far to the north in the spruce forests of Canada, are known to have nested in Bigelow Hollow State Park. One of the smallest birds of the coniferous forests, the golden-crowned kinglet builds its nest from moss, lichens, and even spiderwebs. The inside is lined with feathers and fur, and the nest holds eight or nine cream-colored eggs speckled with brown. This park is one of only two places in Connecticut where both species of kinglets are known to have nested.

Other species that nest in the park include brown creepers, several species of hawks, and pileated woodpeckers. Great-horned, barred, and saw-whet owls also nest in this area.

From the picnic area, I continued along the trail, which follows the western shore of the lake and leads to another favorite spot with huge rock ledges, perfect for sunning or picnicking.

It was late afternoon when I stopped again at Bigelow Pond. The wind had died down, and I watched a red canoe glide silently across the smooth surface of the pond. Three male redstarts were flying through the hemlocks in search of insects. I could understand why, in the West Indies, the Spaniards called these birds "candelitas," for the flashes of bright orange on their wings and tails seemed to light up the dark forest of evergreens. A flock of ducks flew across the pond as the sun dropped below the horizon and the shadows of evening spread across the water.

Winter, when the park's evergreen forests attract evening grosbeaks, pine siskins, and red crossbills, is also a good time for birding. Less frequently seen species include redpolls and pine grosbeaks. Saw-whet owls frequent the pines near Bigelow Pond.

Both of the lakes are popular with fishermen. The waters are stocked with brown and rainbow trout. Boats are limited to 10 mph. The lack of speedboats and development along the shores make both lakes good for canoeing. Mashapaug Lake's hard sand and gravel bottom and clear water attract scuba divers.

Nipmuck State Forest, which covers a total of 8,058 acres, adjoins Bigelow Hollow State Park. Nipmuck Trail passes through the park and also the state forest. You may access the trail off State 171, which is a short distance from the park entrance.

Where: Two miles east of Union on State 197.

Hours: Daily, from 8:00 A.M. to sunset.

Admission: Fee for parking on weekends and holidays from Memorial Day weekend through Labor Day weekend.

Best time to visit: Spring and fall to see birds. For other activities, any season is a good time to visit this park.

Activities: Bird-watching, picnicking, fishing, scuba diving, canoeing, and hiking.

Concessions: None.

Pets: Not permitted near the lakes. Pets on a leash are allowed on the Nipmuck Trail.

For more information: State Parks Division, Bureau of Outdoor Recreation, Connecticut Department of Environmental Protection, 79 Elm Street, Hartford, CT 06106-5127. Call 860-424-3200. Website: www.dep.state.ct.us.

Trail Wood, the Edwin Way Teale Memorial Sanctuary

Located in Hampton, in the rolling country of northeastern Connecticut, is a special place known as Trail Wood, the Edwin Way Teale Memorial Sanctuary. For the last 20 years of his life, Trail Wood was the home of the naturalist, writer, and photographer Edwin Way Teale and his wife, Nellie. Winner of a Pulitzer prize for his four-volume *American Seasons* and the John Burroughs Medal for distinguished nature writing, Teale and his wife had traveled through all the 48 states, yet when it became possible for them to move to the country, it was an old farm outside the small village of Hampton that they chose. One look at the property, and they knew it was the place they had been searching for. If you visit Trail Wood, you will understand why.

The farmhouse, built in 1806 and surrounded by 156 acres of fields, woods, and wetlands, became their home for the next 20 years. These years spent exploring Trail Wood and their observations of its wildlife and plants during all seasons of the year became the subject of Teale's last two books, *A Naturalist Buys an Old Farm* (1974) and *A Walk Through the Year* (1978).

Shortly before Teale's death on October 18, 1980, Edwin and Nellie asked the Connecticut Audubon Society if it would help perpetuate Trail Wood as a wildlife sanctuary. Mrs. Teale retained life tenure of the farmhouse and its immediate environs and continued to live there until her death in 1993.

At present, the trails of the sanctuary are maintained by the Friends of Trail Wood, a local group dedicated to the literary and natural-history legacy of Edwin Way Teale. Their goal is to maintain the trails as they existed during Teale's lifetime and to perpetuate his quest for wildlife preservation and scientific study. All trails are open year-round to the public for nature walks and hiking. Guided walks are part of the schedule of nature programs. The excellent trail map, available from a box near the house, identifies all the points of interest with the names given them by the author and his wife. For the first-time visitor, a guided hike is recommended because there are many intersecting trails that can be confusing. The western boundary is 12,935-acre Natchaug State Forest. Waterproof boots are advisable for the wet season for crossing brooks and wet areas.

Guided hikes often include visiting the naturalist's writing cabin and home. On my first visit to Trail Wood, I was able to join a "Literary Nature Walk" that was part of "Walking Weekend," a three-day event held each October on Columbus Day weekend, which gives participants an opportunity to explore the rich historic, cultural, and natural features in the 25 towns that constitute the Quinebaug and Shetucket River Valley National Heritage Corridor.

When I reached Trail Wood, the meadow parking area was nearly filled to capacity, and I was just in time to join the next walk. For those who treasure Teale's books, there was a sadness associated with seeing the empty house with its great fireplace where on winter evenings Edwin and Nellie liked to sit and read and "feel the warmth of the dancing flames and glowing coals." Some of Teale's marvelous photographs are on the wall of his office and library, where he did much of his writing. The Connecticut Audubon Society now has resident naturalists Jeff Weiler and Annie Guion, who reside at the sanctuary.

In May 1963, four years after moving to Trail Wood, the Teales began the construction of a pond in a swampy area southwest of the house. The pond attracted all kinds of wildlife, and today, it looks as if it had always been part of the landscape. As we followed the trail that Teale had created around the pond, I recalled his observations as he and Nellie watched life come to the pond that first summer. First, there were aquatic insects—water striders and whirligig beetles. Then bullfrogs found a home in the pond, and the first water plants took root. In the evenings, swallows would swoop low over the water to drink.

In the ensuing years, the pond became home for other wildlife. Schools of minnows swam in the shallows, and bluegills and largemouthed bass could be observed from the rustic bridge across Stepping Stone Brook. The fish attracted kingfishers to the pond. In addition to the bullfrogs, five other species of frogs laid their eggs in the Trail Wood pond—the spring peeper, the gray tree frog, the green frog, the pickerel frog, and, on rare occasions, the leopard frog. "Turtle Rock" became the favorite sunning place of painted turtles. The Teales were not the only ones who followed the trail around the pond. On one October morning, they saw a mink on the path, and on another day, Nellie watched a long-tailed weasel hunting beside Driftwood Cove.

The author built a rustic screened-in summerhouse overlooking the pond. Here, on summer evenings, he and Nellie were fond of eating a picnic supper while observing the life around them. Once, after sunset, they watched a great blue heron wading in the shallow water near shore. Just below the summerhouse, they watched robins, catbirds, red-winged blackbirds, grackles, thrushes, and scarlet tanagers bathing in the shallow water. Soon after the pond was built, muskrats came to inhabit it. Watching their activities provided an endless source of fascination during those evenings spent in the summerhouse. Describing their experience, Teale wrote, "We watch these aquatic animals during warm twilights in summer, bringing home food, swimming back and forth across the pond, trailing long ripples, silver V's that grow more silver as the water becomes more dark and mirrorlike."

The pond trail also took us to Teale's writing cabin, a rustic log cabin furnished with a woodstove, oil lamp, desk, and shelves. Teale often came here to read and write, uninterrupted by ringing telephones. Although the cabin is only a five-minute walk from the house, he was surrounded by scenes that reminded him of northern Maine. The pond, only an acre in size, is surrounded by undisturbed woods and hillsides that provide a sanctuary for wildlife. My lasting impression of this walk on the pond trail was of the incredible variety of plants, animals, and birds sustained by this one small pond.

From the pond, we headed north, following the Old Woods Road trail much of the way to the Beaver Pond. This was the Teales' favorite path and the one they most often trod. From the summerhouse, the trail leads north past Woodcock Pasture, where each year, usually in March after the snows melted, Edwin and Nellie would listen with growing anticipation at dusk each day for "the magical flight-song of the woodcock." The trail, which crosses Fern Brook, passes through an area that in summer is filled with cinnamon and interrupted ferns. The leaves of hickories, oaks, and maples made the woods bright with autumn color for our hike. I remember the dark green Christmas ferns carpeting the whole slope of the ridge. In all, 26 species of native ferns grow at Trail Wood, including grape, royal, and sensitive ferns; the silvery spleenwort; the evergreen wood fern; and the New York fern. In addition, several varieties of club mosses carpet the ground.

A trail that crosses Old Woods Road is known as Old Colonial Road. Wagons and carriages, and perhaps even stagecoaches, once rolled over this ancient path.

Finally, we reached the Beaver Pond in the wildest and most northern part of the sanctuary. It was Nellie who, while walking Old Woods Road one early October afternoon, discovered that where a swamp had previously been, there was now a pond covering about three acres. Beavers had blocked the flow of Hampton Brook where it passed through a gap in an old stone wall. Some 30 years later, this original dam, 125 feet long, built of mud and sticks, is still kept in good repair by the industrious inhabitants of the pond. I recalled Teale's description of a memorable night spent beside the pond watching beavers in the moonlight. When I visited the pond, the large old beaver lodge appeared to be abandoned, but a newer lodge toward the north end of the pond showed signs of activity from the freshly cut branches near the entrance. The Beaver Pond has also attracted other wildlife, including frogs, turtles, dragonflies, wood ducks, and Louisiana water thrushes, which Teale observed searching for food in the mud at the edge of the pond.

Following a trail along the edge of the Beaver Pond, we reached "Deerfield." Deer are frequently seen at Trail Wood, especially in this northern part of the sanctuary. One can often find their hoofprints in the moist ground on their trails through the woods. Deer had been seen that morning in a field near the house where, in the fall, they come to eat the fruit of the old apple trees. Teale wrote of finding saplings with the bark removed and the wood polished by bucks rubbing the velvet from their antlers. For Edwin and Nellie, the memory of seeing a magnificent antlered buck seemed "symbolic of all the beauty and wildness of [their] woods."

On the return hike, we followed the Old Colonial Road, and near the top of the ridge, we stopped to examine the stub of a huge chestnut tree. The tree had died in the 1920s from the blight that swept through New England. Today, most chestnut tree seedlings are killed by the blight before they can reach maturity, but there is ongoing research to develop a strain that will be resistant to the blight. We can only hope that someday this magnificent tree can once again grow in New England forests.

Spring is also a good time to visit Trail Wood. In 1974, when *A Naturalist Buys an Old Farm* was published, the bird count for species seen at Trail Wood stood at 144 species. Teale writes about awakening to a dawn chorus of voices that included wood thrushes, veeries, bluebirds, robins, purple finches, catbirds, scarlet tanagers, rose-breasted grosbeaks, and northern orioles. He estimated that between 45 and 50 species of wild birds nested in the woods and fields near the house. In the first day of spring, they would often hear the bluebirds singing in the apple trees. "When we first hear that gentle sound," Teale wrote, "some of the hardness of winter softens within us."

Trail Wood can also be a good destination in winter, when a walk on cross-country skis or snowshoes may reveal animal tracks in the snow. When the Teales were living there, they provided a feeding area for both birds and wild animals. Especially toward the end of winter when food was scarce, the author and his wife would observe gray foxes, skunks, opossums, and raccoons at the feeding area just outside the kitchen door.

Edwin and Nellie Teale never felt as if they owned Trail Wood. They were simply sharing the land with all its other inhabitants. "We are one," Teale wrote, "with the robin among the wild cherries in the sunshine." For them, having the deed to the property conferred responsibility—the responsibility of guardianship—to protect the woods, the streams and fields, and all the wildlife that dwells there. Now that responsibility has passed to others, and other feet walk the familiar trails, perhaps discovering, as the author and his wife did, that "for those who find their pleasure out-of-doors, . . . all the years of existence represent a long love affair with the earth."

Where: From U.S. 6, east of Clark's Corner, turn north on State 97 to Hampton, then west on Kenyon Road to Trail Wood.

Hours: All trails are open year-round from dawn until dusk for unguided nature walks, trail hiking, and nature photography. Contact Trail Wood for information on seasonal activities.

Admission: No admission charge. However, those who wish to help in the maintenance of the sanctuary may join the Friends of Trail Wood or contribute to the Edwin Way Teale Memorial Sanctuary Fund established by the Connecticut Audubon Society in order to help maintain Trail Wood and its wildlife communities.

Best time to visit: Any time of the year is a good time to visit this wonderful area. Edwin and Nellie Teale's years at Trail Wood were devoted to a study of nature's seasonal changes. It is hoped that visitors to Trail Wood, through their explorations and observations, may add to the knowledge about its living communities.

Activities: Nature walks and outdoor study, nature photography, hiking, cross-country skiing, snowshoeing, guided and unguided nature walks, and other programs. Trail Wood also participates in the Connecticut Amphibian Monitoring Program. (See Kellogg Environmental Center for more information on camp.)

Concessions: None.

Pets: Not allowed.

Amenities: There is a toilet facility at the edge of the parking area. However, you need to bring your own supply of drinking water.

For more information: Contact Trail Wood: The Edwin Way Teale Memorial Sanctuary, The Connecticut Audubon Society, 93 Kenyon Road, Hampton, CT 06274. Call 860-455-0759.

Gay City State Park

Located on the Hebron-Bolton town line, along State 85, Gay City State Park is best known for its historical significance as the site of one of Connecticut's early settlements. Gay City was first settled in 1796 by a religious sect led by Elijah Andrus. It was named for John Gay, who became village president in 1800. A sawmill was built on the Blackledge River, and later a woolen mill was constructed on a site one-fourth mile below the present pond. In 1830, the mill was destroyed by fire. A paper mill, built by Dr. Charles Sumner, kept the town alive until the Civil War. When it too caught fire and burned in 1879, it signaled the end of Gay City. Today, white-tailed deer roam what was once the main street of the village; and except for the small graveyard near the park entrance, a few cellar holes, and the remains of the woolen mill, there is little evidence that families once lived here. What man abandoned, nature has reclaimed.

A system of 10 numbered trails connect with each other, making it possible to do a number of loop hikes. Trails connect with the Shenipsit Trail to the west, which runs through Meshomasic and Shenipsit State Forests to the border of Massachusetts. Possum and Partridge Trails are named for the park's wildlife. A trail map is available from the Office of State Parks and Recreation. If you hike in the morning or late afternoon in the spring or fall, there is always the possibility of seeing deer on these forest trails. However, they are wary because hunting is allowed in the adjacent state forests.

In early spring, you may flush a woodcock from a wetland area where there is good cover. A little larger than a quail, this chunky brown bird, with its barred crown and long bill, always looks to me as if it belongs at the edge of the tide on a sand beach. If you are at the park near dusk in late March or early April, you may be fortunate enough to hear the aerial mating song of the male. Only once in spring have I been able to observe this bird in its wild flight. Its magical song begins at the height of its ascent. Then it plunges back to earth, often landing in thick brush in the center of a swamp.

Gay City State Park is also a good place to look for woodland birds such as thrushes, warblers, vireos, chickadees, nuthatches, and woodpeckers. In spring, the woods may resound with the drumming of the male ruffed grouse. The throbbing sound may be repeated, slowly at first, and then with increasing speed until it abruptly stops. The grouse produces the sound by beating its wings. The male drums to call to its mate, to challenge another cock, or sometimes for no reason at all discernible to man. Whatever prompts this display, listening for this sound is for me part of the joy of a hike in Connecticut woods, along with listening for spring peepers, hearing the call of wild geese flying overhead, and catching a glimpse of a white-tailed deer.

The South Trail goes through a wetland area in the southwestern part of the park. After crossing a swampy area on a long boardwalk, the trail climbs gradually to an overlook from which you can look down on an active beaver pond.

A nice sand beach makes the former mill pond a good place to come in summer for swimming and a picnic. Facilities include tables with fireplaces, a rest-room building, and drinking water. The picnic area and rest rooms are accessible to visitors with disabilities.

Gay City State Park is also one of my favorite places to go hiking in the fall. When the oaks and maples along the park road turn to brilliant shades of red and gold, my thoughts go back to that earlier time when this road was the main street of the village. Left off the park road is Gay City Road, once the main route between Gay City and Glastonbury and the Connecticut River, but now a hiking trail where you are likely to encounter small mammals such as chipmunks and gray squirrels as well as woodland birds.

In winter, you can strap on cross-country skis or snowshoes to explore Gay City State Park. The small parking area near the entrance is plowed, and since the park is located just off State 85, it is easily accessible in winter. Moreover, where a trail crosses a stream, the state has built good bridges that facilitate use of the trails in winter. Tracks you are likely to spot in the snow include deer, opossums, squirrels, rabbits, and ruffed grouse. In addition, on any woodland winter walk in Connecticut, there is now the possibility of discovering the tracks of wild turkeys. Since the wild turkey is the largest of our wildfowl, with tracks five inches long, you can easily identify it. The three front toes and the tip of the hind toe off to one side register in the track. The turkeys travel in small flocks of 6 to 12 birds. At night they roost in trees, usually returning each night to the same roosting grounds in wooded bottomlands. Wild turkeys became extinct in Connecticut in 1813 as a result of the destruction of the forests and unregulated hunting. The State Conservation Department began efforts in 1975 to bring the wild turkey back to Connecticut. The effort was so successful that today it is estimated that there are about 20,000 wild turkeys in the state, feeding on a diet of acorns, berries, grass, and insects.

Some people may come to Gay City State Park to look for clues to its vanished past, but for me, its present wildlife and wooded trails and pond hold more interest, making it a favorite place to hike, swim, or cross-country ski.

Where: Three miles south of Bolton on State 85.
Hours: Daily, 8:00 A.M. to sunset, year-round, as conditions permit.
Admission: A parking fee is charged weekends and holidays during the summer season.

Best time to visit: Spring and fall for hiking and viewing wildlife, summer for swimming, winter for cross-country skiing.
Activities: Hiking, horseback riding, picnicking, swimming,
fishing, cross-country skiing, ice skating, exploring a historic
site. No ranger-led activities, but a ranger is on duty during
the summer season. At this time, trail maps are available at the
park.
Concessions: None.
Pets: Not allowed on the beach or in the pond. Pets on a leash
are permitted on wooded hiking trails.
For more information: State Parks Division, Bureau of Outdoor Recreation, Connecticut Department of Environmental
Protection, 79 Elm Street, Hartford, CT 06106-5127. Call
860-424-3200. Website: www.dep.state.ct.us.

Moosup River

The Moosup River, which rises in Rhode Island, flows south
and then west into Connecticut through the towns of Oneco,
Almyville, Moosup, and Central Village, where it joins the
Quinebaug River below Wauregan.

In very early spring, when the water level is high, the central portion of the river from the Almyville Dam
to the State 14 bridge below Central Village offers a 3.5-mile run with class I and
class II rapids for experienced canoeists
able to maneuver around rocks. In this
stretch of the river, the free flow of the water has been blocked
by several dams.

However, when I think of the Moosup River, I think of the
upper reaches and a private family campground, River Bend
Campground, in Oneco, where flocks of wild geese stop to
feed and rest during spring and fall migrations. At George and

Nancy Marchacos's campground, you can pitch your tent in a fragrant grove of white pine trees surrounded by 28 acres of woodlands and open fields. With your own or a rental canoe, you can put in at the campground pond and paddle upstream into Rhode Island. In its upper reaches, the Moosup, at least in summer, is mainly flat water with only a gentle current, which makes it possible to paddle in both directions. Above Oneco, there are no dams. Here the river meanders through isolated, wild, wooded country with extensive marshes that are a haven for many birds, animals, and plants. In Rhode Island, this stretch of river is protected by state forestland in recognition of the river's value to wildlife and to man. On the Connecticut side, the Moosup Valley State Park Trail follows the course of the river for eight miles from Moosup to the Rhode Island state line.

If you canoe upstream, you will pass several cottages. Beyond this point, you paddle for seven miles through unspoiled country toward the river's headwaters. Stained dark brown by the natural tannins in it, the water reflects the clouds overhead and the trees lining the banks. You may find your way blocked by a fallen tree or a beaver dam. That is part of the adventure. As the canoe glides silently along, you may see ducks rising from the marshes or turtles sunning themselves on a partly submerged log. My favorite memory is of a great blue heron that spread its wings and took flight just a short distance ahead of the canoe.

If you stop to explore along the banks of the river, you may find the tracks of deer and raccoons, and gnawed evergreen branches or oval pellets may tell you where a porcupine has been. In addition, many wildflowers grow along the river, including the spectacular red cardinal flower and the wild pink orchid known as the moccasin flower.

The Moosup River is also a fisherman's paradise. It is stocked with trout by both Rhode Island and Connecticut.

Fishing is good for trout, largemouth and smallmouth bass, and pickerel.

Where: From I-395, exit 88, drive 5.5 miles east on State 14A to Oneco. Turn right at the "River Bend" sign just before the bridge.

Hours: River Bend Campground is open April 25 through Columbus Day weekend.

Admission: Overnight, weekly, and seasonal fees for camping. Tent and travel trailers, cabins, canoes, and pedal boats are also rented.

Best time to visit: Late spring, summer, or fall for canoeing and camping. Early mornings or weekdays are the best times for quiet canoe trips to see wildlife.

Activities: Canoeing, camping, fishing, wildlife watching, swimming (pool), and hiking. River Bend Campground also offers complete recreational facilities for families as well as a weekend recreation program. The goal of owners George and Nancy Marchacos is to offer campers a close and personal encounter with natural history. Of special interest is a wildlife exhibit of more than 40 animal mounts.

Kids also have an opportunity to learn about the earth's many treasures at the "River Bend Mining Co.," an interactive attraction where they can mine for gems and minerals from all over the world. Besides having fun, kids have the opportunity to learn to identify more than 125 different minerals, gems, fossils, and shells.

Other facilities: Most campsites have water and electric hookups for RVs, and there are some sites with full hookups. There are also modern rest rooms with hot showers, laundry facilities, and a store. Two rental travel trailers are designed to allow for those in a wheelchair and are equipped with a ramp, handrails, and wider center aisle.

Pets: Pets on a leash are allowed at campsites. However, no pets are allowed when renting a unit (camping trailer or cabin).

For more information: River Bend Campground, Box 23, Route 14A, Oneco, CT 06373. Call 860-564-3440.

For information on the Moosup Valley State Park Trail: State Parks Division, Bureau of Outdoor Recreation, Connecticut Department of Environmental Protection, 79 Elm Street, Hartford, CT 06106-5127. Call 860-424-3200. Website: www.dep.state.ct.us.

5

Southeastern Connecticut

We heard a great horned owl call, far away.
Darkness was coming down the hills.
In the pale water before me,
an otter curved momentarily,
and the silver wake of a beaver flashed,
far down the other lake.

—Florence Page Jaques
Canoe Country

Florence Page Jaques wrote about the vast lake country of northern Minnesota, Ontario, and Manitoba, where the absolute freedom of a canoe trip gives "every hour an intense lucidity." The chain of rivers, lakes, and ponds in southeastern Connecticut, many of which are protected from development by surrounding Pachaug State Forest, is, of course, not comparable in size or isolation to this vast, roadless north country of which Jaques speaks. Yet the experience she describes could easily be repeated on the Pachaug River, where you will often find yourself in wild country.

The landscape changes dramatically as you go south to the coast for a visit to Rocky Neck Park in East Lyme in Connecticut's most celebrated resort area. For wildlife watchers, the best time to visit the southeastern coast of Connecticut is in the spring or fall, when a quiet walk along the beach in search of shorebirds is an especially enjoyable experience.

Pachaug State Forest

One of the most beautiful, unspoiled areas in Connecticut lies within the boundaries of Pachaug State Forest, the state's largest forest, with headquarters in Voluntown. Covering almost 24,000 acres, the forest includes a favorite canoeing stream (the Pachaug River), lakes and ponds that provide excellent fishing, 35 miles of marked hiking trails, 58 campsites, 30 miles of gravel automobile roads, miles of horseback riding trails, and many picnic sites scattered throughout the forest. Pachaug State Forest also contains a unique natural area, a white-cedar swamp where the great rhododendron grows wild and in glorious profusion. It is one of few such areas to be found in New England.

Once the home of the Narragansett, Pequot, and Mohegan Native American tribes, this region was not settled by Europeans until the early 1700s. A tract of land six miles square was granted to the veterans of the Indian Wars. The central part of this area became known as "Volunteers Town," or Voluntown, and was incorporated in 1721. The entire area was farmed and, with the abundant waterpower, many small mills were constructed. Mills for spinning cotton yarn were followed in later years by those for weaving cotton cloth. However, with the development of modern systems of transportation and improved production methods, industrial development moved away from eastern Connecticut. Today, this area of small villages surrounded by state forest lands is a haven for those who enjoy the natural world and outdoor activities.

Pachaug State Forest began with a land purchase in Voluntown in 1928. Today, as you walk through this healthy forest, it is hard to imagine that in the 1920s this forest region was one of the most devastated parts of New England. Trees had been cut again and again without any regard for reforestation, and repeated fires had wreaked more havoc. Extensive plantations of conifers, some of which have now been growing more than 50 years, have helped to restore the forest and attract wildlife. Deer, foxes, raccoons, rabbits, squirrels, pheasants, grouse, and woodcocks may be found here.

To reach the Rhododendron Sanctuary from the center of Voluntown, drive one mile north on State 49. Turn left at the "Forest Headquarters" sign and continue on Headquarters Road to the Mount Misery Recreation Area. There are parking places by a field. To the east of the parking area, a section of the Nehantic Trail winds through the Rhododendron Sanctuary.

This is one walk that you should plan to do between June 15 and July 15. The shrubs generally reach full bloom around July 4. Entering this white-cedar and hemlock swamp forest and seeing for the first time the delicate pink blossoms of this wild rhododendron is an experience unlike any other in Connecticut and one you will never forget. The shrubs tower over your head on either side of the narrow trail, the buds a deeper shade of pink than the blossoms. Tall trunks of white-cedar trees rise from the forest floor, their evergreen crowns filtering the sunlight so that you walk through a cool green world.

Shafts of sunlight fall on the pink blossoms and illumine the dark woods. Here, too, grow tall ferns such as the royal fern and the ostrich fern. Sphagnum moss and bog plants such as sundews, goldthread, and bearberry carpet the ground. In this forest, one feels miles away from civilization. The only sounds I heard were the chattering of a red squirrel and the call of a bird I could not identify. The trail circles back to the road just north of where you left your car.

Mount Misery Campground has 22 wooded sites available on a first-come, first-served basis. Facilities include fireplaces, drinking water, and chemical toilets. There is stream fishing in Mount Misery Brook.

The Mount Misery Area serves as a good base camp for hikers. From here you can hike south on the Nehantic Trail to Green Falls Pond, where there is another campground with 18 wooded sites. Green Falls Pond, with its trout, small islands, and wooded shores lined with rock ledges is a fishing, swimming, and boating paradise. However, the pond is also accessible by auto via Green Falls Road off State 138, so the area may be crowded on summer weekends. Car-top boats may be launched at the pond.

You can also hike north on the Nehantic Trail to Hopeville Pond State Park for swimming and camping. The total distance of this trail is about 14 miles.

From Mount Misery Campground, you can gain access to the Pachaug Trail, which joins the Nehantic Trail east of Headquarters Road near the ccc Youth Area. You can hike for 30 miles on the Pachaug Trail through rugged country, passing streams, ponds, and rock formations, and continue on into the Arcadia Management Area of southwestern Rhode Island, all without leaving state-owned land. It is indeed fortunate that two relatively small and developed states have had the foresight to preserve this large area from development. It benefits man, by providing endless opportunities for outdoor recreation and nature study, and wildlife, by offering an almost continuous tract of land where commercial development does not intrude.

Maps of the recreation areas and trails in Pachaug State Forest are available from the State Parks Division of the Department of Environmental Protection. The Mount Misery Area is part of the Herman Haupt Chapman Management Area. On May 21, 1966, 2,000 acres of Pachaug State Forest were dedicated as a memorial to Chapman, a professor at the Yale School of Forestry, for his interest in the preservation of Connecticut's natural resources.

Just south of the "Forest Headquarters" sign on State 49 is the state boat-launching area, which is restricted to fishing and the launching of boats on the Pachaug River. There is space for parking, and those who use a wheelchair will find a ramp and fishing platform overlooking the river. Largemouth bass and yellow perch are the species most often caught here.

A gentle, copper-colored ribbon of water, the Pachaug River winds its way through the forest. Part of a chain of lakes and ponds, the river flows for many miles through wild country and small villages. From the launching area, you can canoe downstream into Beachdale Pond, a shallow body of water with extensive marshes, where you have a good chance of seeing painted turtles. You can also canoe upstream on the Pachaug, past a private campground, Nature's Campsites, which has large wooded sites, some of them right along the river. Canoe rentals are available to campers. In all, an 11.5-mile canoe trip is possible on the Pachaug River through the chain of lakes and ponds from Doaneville Pond off State 138 through Glasgo Pond, Pachaug Pond, Hopeville Pond, and Ashland Pond, where the Pachaug joins the Quinebaug River, another good flat-water canoeing stream. Wildlife you might see on a canoe trip include black ducks, wood ducks, and kingfishers. Toward evening you're likely to see signs of beaver activity or catch a glimpse of a deer coming to the edge of the river or a pond to drink.

Where: The entrance to Pachaug State Forest (Mount Misery Area and State Forest Headquarters) is one mile north of the center of Voluntown on State 49.

Hours: Recreation areas in Pachaug State Forest are open for day use year-round, as conditions permit, from 8:00 A.M. to sunset. The official camping season begins in mid-April and ends September 30. Check with Forest Headquarters if you want to camp before or after these dates.

Admission: At Green Falls Pond, there is a charge for parking, weekends and holidays during the summer season. A daily fee is also charged for camping permits.

Best time to visit: The Rhododendron Sanctuary should be visited between June 15 and July 15 in order to see the shrubs in bloom. Otherwise, any season, except during hunting season, is a good time for exploring this vast state forest.

Activities: Hiking, viewing unique natural delights, canoeing, swimming, camping (also horse camp area at Frog Hollow Horse Camp), fishing, horseback riding, cross-country skiing, snowshoeing, dog-sled racing.

Concessions: At nearby Hopeville Pond State Park in Griswold, North American Canoe Tours rents canoes at Hopeville Pond, which is actually part of the Pachaug River that has been widened for a distance of three miles. Canoes are available from Memorial Day through Labor Day.

Pets: Pets on a leash are allowed on state-forest trails and in picnic areas. They are also allowed at the three campgrounds, where they are limited to one per campsite and must be on a leash not to exceed seven feet in length. Dogs must have proof of rabies vaccination.

Other: In addition to the campgrounds at Green Falls Pond

and in the Mount Misery Area, there is Frog Hollow Horse Camp, designed specifically for equestrian use. The campground has 18 semiwooded sites, which are available on a first-come, first-served basis. The season extends from April 15 through Thanksgiving.

Besides the state campgrounds and Nature's Campsites, open May 1 to October 15, another private campground in Voluntown that will appeal to those who enjoy nature-related activities is Ye Olde Countryside Campground, also open from May to October, with unusually large sites shaded by pines and oaks. Some sites have rock ledges, and many overlook the pond, where campers enjoy fishing and swimming.

For more information: Pachaug State Forest, P.O. Box 5, Voluntown, CT 06384. Call 860-376-4075.

State Parks Division, Bureau of Outdoor Recreation, Department of Environmental Protection, 79 Elm Street, Hartford, CT 06106-5127. Call 860-424-3200. Website: www. dep.state.ct.us. (for maps and general information on state camping areas).

Nature's Campsites, Route 49-N, Voluntown, CT 06384. Call 860-376-4203.

Ye Olde Countryside Campground, 75 Cook Hill Road, Voluntown, CT 06384. Call 860-376-0029.

North American Canoe Tours, Inc., 65 Black Point Road, Niantic, CT 06357. Call 860-739-0791.

Rocky Neck State Park

A white sand beach on Long Island Sound brings hundreds of visitors to Rocky Neck State Park in East Lyme each summer. The warm, clear water and gently sloping beach, along with campsites within walking distance of the beach, make the park a favorite destination for family vacations. Since the park is crowded in summer, the best times for nature and bird walks are in spring, fall, and even winter.

That this fine recreational area was set aside as a public park was due to the foresight of a few conservationists led by Henry Graves and Albert M. Turner, who in 1931 used their own personal funds to hold the land until they were recompensed by the state legislature.

The 561-acre park is bounded on the west by Four Mile River, a tidal river, and on the east by a broad salt marsh. The entrance road runs along the border of the marsh, and if you drive this road in spring or fall, you have a good chance of seeing great blue herons, black ducks, green-winged teal, and mallards. Rocky Neck State Park is also a good place to see ospreys, which visit there in early summer.

Bride Brook also flows through the park, and in March and April high spring tides allow great schools of alewives (herring) to swim into Bride Brook on a journey to their inland spawning grounds. There is a crabbing and handicapped-accessible fishing area on the brook where the entrance road crosses the stream, just before the first parking area.

The attractive campground can be found near the park entrance. Five separate areas, named after shorebirds, have a total of 160 wooded and open sites. There are separate tenting areas near a nature center. Facilities include modern rest rooms with showers. Individual fireplaces are not provided. Those who bring bicycles will find a bikeway that connects the camping area with the park road near the first parking area.

A large pavilion of native fieldstone, which was built mostly by hand during the 1930s, overlooks the beach and a stone fishing jetty. Pillars supporting the pavilion were cut from trees in each of the state parks and state forests. On cool or rainy days, picnickers and campers gather around the pavilion's large fireplaces.

Hiking trails in the park consist of a main circular trail marked with white blazes and side trails marked with yellow blazes that lead to places with intriguing names like Baker's Cave, Tony's Nose, and Shipyard. Hikers should park in the first large parking area to the right of the entrance. Here trail maps are available. The trail starts at a white blaze near the far corner of the lot and crosses a marsh, where you may see ducks. Beyond the marsh, you enter woods where, depending on the season, you may find mountain laurel in bloom or ripe blueberries. The trail affords views of the Four Mile River and Long Island Sound before ending at the beach.

Saltwater fishing is a popular pastime either from the jetty or the beach. Depending on the time of year, you can fish for mackerel, striped bass, or flounder.

Where: Take exit 72 off I-95 and follow the signs east to the park, which is located off State 156 in East Lyme.

Hours: Open for day use year-round, as conditions permit, from 8:00 A.M. to sunset. The camping season extends from mid-April to September 30. However, check first with the State Parks Division if you want to camp before Memorial Day or after Labor Day.

Admission: There is a daily parking fee during the summer season. A fee is also charged weekends only from mid-April through mid-May, and again from the weekend following Labor Day through the end of September. A nightly fee is charged for each campsite.

Best time to visit: Spring, fall, and winter are the best times as the park is crowded in summer.

Activities: Swimming, scuba diving, hiking, camping, bird-watching, picnicking, bicycling, saltwater fishing, interpretive programs, and cross-country skiing. Picnicking, camping, and fishing facilities are accessible to visitors with disabilities.

Concessions: During the summer months, a food concession operates and is accessible to visitors with disabilities.

Pets: Not allowed on the beach or in the camping area.

For more information: Rocky Neck State Park, Box 676, Niantic, CT 06357. Call park office, 860-739-5471; campground office, 860-739-1339.

State Parks Division, Bureau of Outdoor Recreation, Department of Environmental Protection, 79 Elm Street, Hartford, CT 06106-5127. Call 860-424-3200. Website: www. dep.state.ct.us.

RHODE ISLAND

6

Inland

Our village life would stagnate
if it were not for the unexplored forests
and meadows which surround it.
We need the tonic of wilderness. . . .

—HENRY DAVID THOREAU
Walden

Not only is Rhode Island the smallest state, but its population density is exceeded only by that of New Jersey.
These facts help explain the pressures for development that
threaten the state's natural areas. Nevertheless, most citizens
of Rhode Island live entirely in cities, and the western part of
the state remains a rural area with forests, glacial bogs,
streams, ponds, and freshwater swamps that provide a home
for wildlife as well as a refuge for people—places where you
can hike or swim or paddle a canoe and hear only the sounds
of birds or the call of a bullfrog from a forested swamp.

Fortunately, a coalition of state and private organizations is
working to protect Rhode Island's natural areas. Large tracts
of land have been set aside as state parks and forests. In addition, three private organizations—the Audubon Society of
Rhode Island, the Heritage Trust of Rhode Island, and The

Nature Conservancy—are working together along with local private land trusts for the purpose of protecting land and the wildlife and plant life found there. The Audubon Society of Rhode Island manages more than 8,000 acres, tracts of land that are important because they provide critical habitat or offer special natural features. The Heritage Trust of Rhode Island holds both natural areas and historical sites, and The Nature Conservancy owns or controls about 800 acres in eight wildlife habitat preserves for endangered species in Rhode Island.

Preserving the forests and meadows while protecting the ponds and streams of interior Rhode Island will ensure that the "tonic of wilderness" will always be there.

Casimir Pulaski Memorial State Park

Situated in northwestern Rhode Island, Casimir Pulaski Memorial State Park, surrounded by 3,200 acres of the George Washington Management Camping Area, is one of Rhode Island's most picturesque state parks. Located off U.S. 44 just east of the Rhode Island state line, the park attracts many visitors in the summer with its long sandy beach and inviting warm-water swimming and fishing in Peck Pond. However, on a Sunday afternoon in August, I did not find the park overly crowded. There was plenty of space to enjoy a swim and picnic, and while hiking around the pond, I met only two other persons. What makes this park attractive, in addition to the pond, is the rolling hilly terrain with rocks and ledges, fragrant pine woods, and ground carpeted with ferns, wintergreen, and blueberries.

Following the trail around the edge of the pond, I came upon several quiet fishing spots. One was a broad rock ledge that reached to the water's edge. Kids love to fish here and enjoy the thrill of a tug on the line even if it turns out to be only a sunfish.

For a longer hike, a trail leads east and in about a quarter-mile connects with the Walkabout Trail in the George Washington Management Camping Area. This trail actually consists of three overlapping loop trails, on which you can walk from two to eight miles. Trail maps are available from the Forestry Headquarters in Chepachet. New Englanders can thank Australia for this fine hiking trail. In 1965, while an Australian ship, the *Perth*, was in dry dock in Newport, her crew volunteered its services to build a hiking trail.

The eight-mile loop takes you through a forest of magnificent hemlocks and along an earthen dam built to create a marsh. Here, nesting boxes have been put out to attract wood ducks. In addition to these colorful ducks, you might see muskrats, which also inhabit this marsh.

In about five miles, you come to Bowdish Reservoir and the George Washington Management Camping Area, with 45 sites and two shelters in a wooded area overlooking the lake. The camping area, also accessible from U.S. 44, is heavily used by those who come to swim, launch boats, and fish for largemouth bass, yellow perch, and pickerel. Water-based recreation, including waterskiing, is heavy on the reservoir during the summer months, and the southwestern end has a good deal of private development.

The creation of Bowdish Reservoir unfortunately destroyed a large bog. Today, the only remnants of this bog are a few floating islands, which still support some rare bog plants and sundews. Although you won't find solitude here, the reservoir is still a good destination for an enjoyable canoe trip in spring and fall. Paddle along the eastern shore and you'll find plenty of places to go ashore in the George Washington Management Camping Area. However, the islands are in the center of the reservoir, and if there is wind, sizable waves can build up on this rather large body of water. Use caution when paddling out into open water.

Continuing the loop hike will take you through more groves of hemlock and along the shore of Wilbur Pond back to your starting point and the side trail back to Peck Pond. During this hike, you have a good chance of spotting woodland songbirds such as thrushes, flycatchers, and warblers. You may also hear the familiar call of the quail, or "bobwhite," or, in spring, listen to the drumming of the ruffed grouse. Deer, raccoons, rabbits, and squirrels also inhabit these woods.

Where: Casimir Pulaski Memorial State Park in West Glocester is reached via a left turn on Pulaski Road, just over the state line from Connecticut, on U.S. 44 east. Turn at the sign for "Pulaski Recreation Area."

The George Washington Management Camping Area is also off U.S. 44, two miles east of the Connecticut state line.

Hours: Casimir Pulaski Memorial State Park is open for day use from 5:00 A.M. until one-half hour after sunset, year-round.

Camping is available in the George Washington Management Camping Area from the second weekend in April to October 15. Permits are issued by the park ranger on a first-come, first-served basis.

Admission: There is no fee charged for parking at Casimir Pulaski Memorial State Park. There is, however, a nightly fee for camping permits.

Best time to visit: Spring and fall for hiking, camping, canoeing, and bird-watching. Although the park may be crowded in summer, it is still an enjoyable place for a picnic and swimming. In the winter, the park is open for ice skating and cross-country skiing.

Activities: In both Casimir Pulaski Memorial State Park and George Washington Management Camping Area—swimming, hiking, picnicking, fishing, bird-watching, and cross-country skiing. George Washington Managemnet Camping Area, in addition to camping, has a boat-launching area. In winter, Peck Pond in Casimir Pulaski Memorial State Park offers skating. During the summer season, lifeguards are on duty and park rangers are available to answer questions.

Concessions: None.

Amenities: Facilities at Casimir Pulaski Memorial State Park include bathhouses, rest rooms, and a covered picnic pavilion.

Pets: Pets are not allowed on the beach or in the camping area. Otherwise, pets on a leash are permitted.

For more information: Rhode Island Department of Environmental Management, Division of Forest Environment, 2185 Putnam Pike, Chepachet, RI 02814. Call 401-568-2013.

Powder Mill Ledges Wildlife Refuge

Powder Mill Ledges Refuge, a wildlife sanctuary of the Audubon Society of Rhode Island, covers 81 acres and is situated just off busy U.S. 44 in Smithfield. The Audubon Society headquarters is also located here.

Founded in 1897, the Audubon Society of Rhode Island, an independent state organization, even in its earliest years recognized the importance of conservation of natural habitats to protect birds and other wildlife and plants. Today, the society manages more than 8,000 acres in Rhode Island, retaining most of the woodlands and wetlands in their natural state for wildlife habitat and/or watershed protection. Seven of the 65 properties operate as education centers, with groomed trails and programs and walks led by professional naturalists. Powder Mill Ledges Wildlife Refuge is one of the properties that has been developed for public use.

This upland woodland refuge is notable for its stands of northern red oak, white pine, and pitch pine and for its small pond and wetlands, which attract many species of wildlife. For those who walk its trails, it is a refuge from the spreading commercial and residential development along heavily traveled U.S. 44.

The land has a long history of use. The original forest was cut to provide lumber for homes, carriages, and ships. In the 1800s, it was part of a dairy farm, and cows grazed on what was then a treeless hillside pasture. When you walk the trails today, you will see the old stone walls that were part of the farm. The refuge takes its name from a powder mill that was built in the area, although the exact location remains unknown. By the early 1900s, the land was already returning to forest. Many species of wildflowers were recorded, and the pond attracted ducks and herons.

The refuge features three loops of trails. Before starting out to walk the trails, stop at the headquarters building to register and pick up a trail map and a guide to the orange loop trail. The building also houses the Hathaway Library of Natural History and an excellent book and gift shop. Available for purchase for a small fee is a "Properties Map," which will serve as a guide to the other Audubon refuges open to the public. It also includes a chart listing all the Audubon Society of Rhode Island properties and their features.

The entrance to the orange marked trail is near the headquarters building. The sound of traffic fades as you enter a section of the woodland where you pass a sugar maple, quaking aspens, red maples, and red oaks. Along the edge of a field, nesting boxes for tree swallows and eastern bluebirds crown the fence posts.

Continuing along the trail, you reach a forested swamp, which sits in a depression formed by the last glacier. This swamp is undergoing the process of natural succession: what was once open water evolved into a marsh, and then a shrub swamp, before it became a forested swamp. Most of the trees here are red maples. Many kinds of birds are attracted to this area—more than 150 species have been recorded in the refuge. The swamp and small pond are also home to a variety of frogs, such as wood and green frogs, turtles, and aquatic insects. As I approached the pond, I heard the calls of bullfrogs and saw painted turtles sunning themselves on a partly submerged log. A walk by the pond may even reward you with the sight of a great blue heron or a muskrat.

Before passing through a high stone wall built by farmers long ago, look for three kinds of ferns on the left: cinnamon fern, sensitive fern, and lady fern. The refuge is also a good place to test your wildflower identification skills. In late spring and early summer, many plants that have thrived here since the early days of this century are in bloom. See if you can spot jack-in-the-pulpit, pipsissewa, downy rattlesnake plantain, pink lady's slipper, Indian cucumber root, false Solomon's seal, true Solomon's seal, wild geranium, and Turk's-cap lilies.

The trail then continues uphill through a fragrant white-pine forest. After grazing ended on this hillside pasture, pine seedlings began to take over the field. Some large hardwoods have also grown up, but it is the sweet scent of the pine woods that you will remember.

The fields of the refuge, which provide food for many seed-eating birds and mammals, including mice and woodchucks, are mowed only once every two years. Goldenrod, joe-pye weed, sensitive fern, and wetland grasses grow here. Wildlife food patches, such as rye grass and sunflowers, have been planted to supplement the winter food supply within the refuge. Song sparrows and other field species would lose their habitat if the fields were allowed to return to forest.

Despite human intrusion in the form of a shopping center bordering the refuge, spring peepers and American toads still use the wetland at the end of the parking area, and their calls can be heard on a spring evening. Trees planted along the boundary line to act as a buffer provide additional habitat for such birds as catbirds, mockingbirds, and robins.

Back at the headquarters building, a bird-feeding area with a bird blind nearby lets photographers and bird-watchers view the birds without disturbing them. Along the side of the building, next to the bird blind, is a butterfly garden with flowers that supply nectar for butterflies to feed on as well as plants that certain caterpillars need for food.

This sanctuary demonstrates how home owners can make even a small property more hospitable to wildlife by planting shrubs and trees for cover and food and by replacing part of the lawn with a section of wildflowers and grasses. Even on a small lot, you can plant a butterfly garden and put out bird feeders in winter to supplement the natural supply of food.

Where: From exit 7B on I-295, drive west one mile to U.S. 44, then 0.1 mile south on State 5. The headquarters building and parking lot at 12 Sanderson Road in Smithfield will be on your left after you make the turn at this busy intersection.
Hours: Trails are open from dawn to dusk. The headquarters building, with its library and book and gift shop, is open weekdays from 9:00 A.M. to 5:00 P.M. and on Saturday from noon to 4:00 P.M.; closed holidays.

Admission: A nominal fee may be charged to defray maintenance costs. Fees are charged for special programs, but members of the Audubon Society of Rhode Island can attend programs at reduced rates.

Best time to visit: Spring and fall to see birds, late spring and early summer for wildflowers, winter for cross-country skiing.

Activities: Nature walks to observe and learn about wildlife, including bird-watching, and about wildflowers and other plants. (A self-guided tour on one of the trails can be used to learn to identify many species of plants and trees.) Photographing plants, birds, and animals. In winter snow, cross-country skiing and snowshoeing. Exhibits, films, educational programs, and walks led by professional naturalists. (See Prudence Island for programs offered in the Narragansett Bay National Estuarine Research Reserve by the Audubon Society of Rhode Island.)

Pets: Not allowed.

Other: Picnicking is not allowed here. Nearby Pulaski Memorial State Park is a good place to have your lunch.

For more information: Audubon Society of Rhode Island, 12 Sanderson Road (Route 5), Smithfield, RI 02917-2606. Call 401-949-5454.

Roger Williams Park Zoo

Those interested in zoos and the preservation of endangered species will also want to visit Roger Williams Park Zoo in Providence, Rhode Island. In fact, in developing a master plan for Beardsley Zoo in Connecticut, it was this neighboring zoological park that served as a model. Considered one of the best zoos in the country for its conservation efforts and winner of two national Significant Achievement Awards from the American Zoo and Aquarium Association, Roger Williams

Park Zoo is a leading participant in the global Species Survival Plan, which seeks to save endangered species from extinction through the captive breeding program.

Visitors will find more than 160 species of rare and fascinating animals and birds exhibited in expansive natural settings. Spending a day at this zoo can include a safari on the "Plains of Africa," where you'll see zebras, elephants, cheetahs, and giraffes. In the Tropical America building, you can view rain forest monkeys from a canopy skywalk. Underwater viewing exhibits offer the whole family a chance to observe the hidden worlds of polar bears, otters, and baby alligators.

The Marco Polo Trail exhibit, which opened in 1996, follows the route of the explorer across Asia and combines animals, botany, history, and culture into an exciting interactive experience, the first of its kind in the United States.

A new exhibit, which opened in 1998, takes visitors into the hidden and often misunderstood world of the bat and offers an opportunity to learn about these fascinating mammals.

Roger Williams Park Zoo is operated and maintained by the City of Providence Parks Department, and supported by the Rhode Island Zoological Society.

Where: From I-95 south bound, take exit 17 (Elmwood Avenue). Turn left at the light, and take your second left into the park. Follow signs to the zoo entrance. From I-95 north bound, take exit 16. Bear right and turn left at the light. The park is one-half block on the right. Follow signs to the zoo entrance.

Hours: Roger Williams Park is open daily from 7:00 A.M. to 9:00 P.M. The zoo is open every day except Christmas, weekdays from 9:00 A.M. to 5:00 P.M. (Saturday, Sunday, and holidays from 9:00 A.M. to 6:00 P.M.), April through October, and from 9:00 A.M. to 4:00 P.M. the rest of the year.

Admission: An admission fee is charged. Senior citizens and children ages 3 to 12 pay a reduced rate. Children under 3 are admitted free.

Best time to visit: A spring or fall visit avoids the crowds associated with the busy summer months.

Activities: In addition to visiting the various exhibits, the zoo has two restaurants (Alice's Restaurant and the Hungry Bear Cafe) and a gift shop stocked with fun and educational items. Roger Williams Park includes extensive flower gardens, an amphitheater for outdoor concerts, a planetarium, and a Museum of Natural History with wildlife displays and interactive exhibits. Carousel Village features a vintage carousel.

Pets: Not allowed.

For more information: Roger Williams Park and Zoo, 1000 Elmwood Ave., Providence, RI 02907. Call 401-785-3510.

Arcadia Management Area

Located north of Hope Valley in the southwestern part of Rhode Island, the Arcadia Management Area, which encompasses 14,000 acres of state-owned land, is one of the largest remaining natural areas in this smallest state in the Northeast. Visitors will find recreation areas at Beach Pond and Browning Mill Pond (also known as Arcadia Park), miles of hiking trails, several ponds, trout streams, and delightful views.

You can reach this area easily from State 165, which traverses the heart of the state forest. Beach Pond, a large body of water that stretches across the state line into Connecticut, is on State 165. The parking area is in Exeter, Rhode Island. Beach Pond Recreation Area shares a two-mile-long beach with Pachaug State Forest in Connecticut. The long sandy beach and clear water make this a popular spot for swimming and boating, and it is likely to be crowded during the summer. One of Rhode Island's most memorable hiking trails, the Hemlock Ledges Trail, which is part of the Tippecansett Trail, begins at the beach parking area and follows along the shore of the pond. From the summit of the ledges, you see all of Beach Pond.

As you head east on State 165, the landscape varies from gently rolling hills to level stretches of scrub oak and pine reminiscent of Cape Cod. A right turn on Arcadia Road will take you to the Browning Mill Pond Recreation Area. Here on a warm summer day, the crescent-shaped beach is an ideal destination. The sand is soft, the water is warm and shallow, and there is a safe, roped-off wading area for children. Fishing for pickerel and smallmouth and largemouth bass is a favorite pastime.

The picnic area at Browning Mill Pond is outstanding. Some of the tables are scattered along the shore of the pond and on a wooded peninsula, while others are close to Roaring Brook or in a quiet expanse beneath tall trees. Many sites have fireplaces. Just beyond the beach, in the upper picnic area near the pavilion, Roaring Brook cascades through the woods, dropping into clear, shallow pools that delight children. The covered picnic pavilion is available for group use by reservation only.

On a warm weekday in mid-July, I found the beach and picnic areas uncrowded. Most of the swimmers had opted for the larger beach and deeper water at Beach Pond. I found my favorite picnic site unoccupied. Situated on a point of land extending into the pond, it captures a restful view and the shade of tall pine trees. I ate lunch while cooling my feet in the water and enjoying the breeze.

Since I was last in Arcadia Park, a small flock of Canada geese had taken up residence at the pond. Depending on how you feel about sharing a swimming beach with geese, this can be viewed as either a positive or a negative feature; but watching them swim in the shallow water among the water lilies, I could not help but feel that they belonged here.

The Arcadia Management Area offers 30 miles of hiking trails that are maintained by the Narragansett Chapter of the Appalachian Mountain Club. Views and wildlife are abundant. Hikers report seeing deer, foxes, otter, beaver, raccoons, and coyotes.

After lunch I hiked a section of the Arcadia Trail that begins at the Dawley State Park Picnic Area off State 3 and traverses a wooded area with mature stands of beech trees before it reaches Arcadia Park and follows the shore of Browning Mill Pond. Along the shore of the pond, tall shrubs border the trail. In July, I found the fragrant pink blossoms of wild honeysuckle and a few ripe high-bush blueberries. Earlier in the season, mountain laurel had been in bloom. Tall oaks, maples, hickories, and white pine are the predominant trees. Ferns and club mosses carpet the ground. Large boulders are scattered about the hilly terrain, and stone walls testify that this was once farming country.

Backpack camping is available by permit only at the Stepstone Falls Camping Area, where the Falls River flows over a series of wide, flat rocks that resemble giant steps. Four campsites are available on a first-come, first-served basis. The camping area is located between the Tippecansett and Ben Utter Trails.

A special campground for persons with horses is located on Escoheag Hill Road, north of State 165. Permits are issued at the area with a four-night maximum stay allowed.

The Mount Tom Trail begins along State 165 about 2.5 miles west of State 3. In less than one mile, it reaches a parking area on the Wood River, a favorite with trout fishermen and canoeists. The trail then passes through a pine forest planted after a fire destroyed more than 7,000 acres of forestland in 1951. The pines now serve as a resting area for warblers during migration periods. In a little more than two miles from the start of this hike, the trail ascends to rock ledges from which there is a panoramic view of the forested valleys below. The trail continues on to the forested summit, but the views are best from the ledges.

A brochure describing the hiking trails is available from the Department of Environmental Management. Many of the trails in the Arcadia Management Area are linked to trails in Pachaug State Forest in Connecticut. For hikers and wildlife watchers, this means that an area of more than 36,000 acres has been set aside for the benefit of man and wildlife, an area where maintaining the natural environment and protecting the quality of natural resources are the primary goals.

Where: From Voluntown, Connecticut, drive east on State 165. Beach Pond Recreation Area is on State 165. Parking is on the left just over the Rhode Island border.

To reach the Browning Mill Pond Recreation Area, continue driving east on State 165. About six miles from the Rhode Island state line, and shortly after passing a sign and entrance road on the left for the Arcadia Management Headquarters, turn right on an unmarked road known as Arcadia Road. Although there was no road or park sign when I was there, it is the only wide paved road running south from State 165. If you miss the turn, you will reach the intersection of State 3 after one mile. By turning around and going west on State 165, you can then take your first left. Parking for the Browning Mill Pond Recreation Area will be on your right. From there, it is a short walk down the hill to the pond and beach.

Hours: The Arcadia Management Area is open for day use from 5:00 A.M. until one hour after sunset. Pond and stream fishing is allowed when the area is closed for other activities. Permits for backpack camping must be obtained in person. During the summer season, the park office at Browning Mill Pond is normally open daily from 8:30 A.M. to 4:00 P.M. At other times, permits will be issued from the Division of Forest Environment Headquarters on Arcadia Road, weekdays only, from 8:30 A.M. to 4:00 P.M.

Admission: A fee is charged for parking at the Beach Pond Recreation Area during the summer season. No fee for use of the Browning Mill Pond Recreation Area. Campers pay a fee for permits to camp at the Stepstone Falls Camping Area and at Legrand G. Reynolds Horsemen's Camping Area on Escoheag Hill Road.

Best time to visit: Spring, summer, and early fall are good times to explore the Arcadia Management Area. With the exception of Beach Pond on summer weekends, the area is not likely to be overcrowded. Spring, during the warbler migration, and September are special times to visit this area. Because hunting is allowed in State Management Areas, it is best to avoid this area from the second weekend in October through the last day in February. During hunting season, state regulations require that all users of State Management Areas wear at least 200 square inches of daylight fluorescent orange. An orange hat or vest will fulfill the requirement.

Activities: Hiking, swimming, picnicking, fishing, canoeing, kayaking, wildlife watching, horseback riding, backpack and horsemen's camping.

Concessions: None.

Pets: No dogs are allowed on beaches or in camping areas. Dogs on a leash, not more than 25 feet long, are allowed in picnic areas and on trails.

Other: For family camping, two private campgrounds are located in West Greenwich, surrounded by acres of state forest lands for hiking, swimming, and boating. Oak Embers

Campground, open from February to December, has 60 shaded sites for tents and RVs, several Adirondack-style shelters, a camp store, swimming pool, and game room. Peeper Pond Campground in Exeter has 31 wooded tent and trailer sites in a quiet natural setting with a limited camp store.

For more information: Rhode Island Department of Environmental Management, Division of Forest Environment, Arcadia Headquarters, 260 Arcadia Road, Hope Valley, RI 02832. Call 401-539-2356.

Legrand G. Reynolds Horsemen's Camping Area, 260 Arcadia Road, Hope Valley, RI 02832. Call 401-539-2356.

Oak Embers Campground, 219 Escoheag Hill Road, West Greenwich, RI 02817. Call 401-397-4042.

Peeper Pond Campground, P.O. Box 503, Exeter, RI 02822. Call 401-294-5540.

7

The Coast

There is nothing so small, nothing so great,
That it does not respond to those celestial spring days,
and give the pendulum of life a fresh start.

—JOHN BURROUGHS
Birds and Poets

It was in the spring that I spent a day at Ninigret Conservation Area, on a day when the long sandy beach belonged to the birds and to those who came to watch them. No place in Rhode Island is more than 25 miles from the sea. Unlike Connecticut, where the coast is sheltered by the long arm of Long Island, Rhode Island's coast faces the open Atlantic, but along its shores are salt ponds and marshes protected from the open ocean by barrier beaches. The ponds serve as a nursery and feeding ground for a great variety of birds and shellfish, and protected coastal ponds and marshes serve as a refuge for birds and waterfowl during seasonal migrations.

Narragansett Bay cuts deeply into the land. With its many islands, coves, and channels, it invites endless exploration both by land and by sea.

I hope that the following pages will serve as an introduction to the natural wonders of coastal Rhode Island. Those who spend time here will discover many other special places.

Ninigret National Wildlife Refuge and Conservation Area

The Ninigret National Wildlife Refuge occupies a 404-acre tract of coastal plain near Charlestown. It borders the northern end of Ninigret Pond, which is four miles long and half a mile wide at its broadest point. The Ninigret Conservation Area is a barrier beach more than two miles long. No vehicles are allowed in the refuge, and the only access to the Conservation Area is via East Beach Road. When you reach the beach, turn left, drive past some cottages, and you will see the entrance signs and parking area for Ninigret Conservation Area. From here, you have access to the shore of Ninigret Pond and the barrier beach. Visit this area in fall or spring because in summer the beach attracts crowds and the parking lot is closed when it is filled to capacity.

On a cool day in mid-May, when the sun was having a hard time breaking through the clouds, I found an almost deserted beach. Only two other persons were braving the cool breeze and threat of showers to walk beside the waves. Just as I reached the ocean, the sun broke through the clouds, illuminating everything with a magical light that lasted several moments. A small flock of terns had alighted on the beach, and a lone piping plover was working the edge of the incoming waves. Ducks flew overhead, and a great black-backed gull appeared to be the sentinel of the beach. I could see Block Island 12 miles away and a couple of fishing boats.

You can walk this beach for a distance of over two miles as far as the Charlestown Breachway, which connects Ninigret Pond with the Atlantic Ocean. During a walk along this beach in spring or fall, you are likely to see sandpipers, plovers, and willets feeding at the edge of the tide, and ducks, including canvasbacks and goldeneyes, riding the waves offshore. On a nice day, you can enjoy the sunshine, the ocean, and the birds, and the only sounds you are apt to hear are the waves breaking on the beach and the cry of gulls overhead.

From the parking area, it is just a few steps to the shore of Ninigret Pond, the largest in a string of ponds along the southern Rhode Island shore. Sign boards inform the visitor that this salt pond is a rich environment that is both a nursery and a feeding ground for shellfish, finfish, and birds. Because the salt water is diluted with fresh water from streams and springs, the pond can nourish brackish species like oysters as well as creatures of the sea such as quahogs, soft-shelled clams, and flounder. Flounder lay their eggs in Ninigret Pond during the winter; the young hatch and remain in the pond, feeding for two or three years. Aquatic vegetation flourishes in ponds like Ninigret, which has an average depth of only four feet. The plant nutrients provide a rich source of food for finfish and shellfish. Salt ponds play a vital role. In serving as nurseries, they supply the ocean with many varieties of fish. Ninigret Pond, along with adjoining Green Hill Pond, supply Block Island Sound with as much as one-quarter of its winter flounder. The pond also attracts black ducks, which feed on the abundant eelgrass, and mallards, which nest along the banks each year. Mute swans also nest and raise their young along the edges of the pond.

In addition to hiking along the beach, you have a wide choice of other activities in the area. There are hiking trails within the federal refuge—a map is posted at Foster Cove off

U.S. 1—and you can also hike on Grassy Point, which is accessible from Ninigret Park off State 1A in Charlestown. Ninigret Park is a recreational park with a swimming pond, picnic grounds, a ten-speed bike course, ballfields, and tennis and basketball courts situated on 227 acres. The Frosty Drew Memorial Nature Center, also located in the park near the refuge entrance, has an observatory and trails. It is open during the summer months and offers displays, interpretive programs, and nature-related activities for children. Trail maps and information can also be obtained there.

The checklist of bird species for the Ninigret National Wildlife Refuge, which includes satellite refuges at Trustom Pond, Sachuest Point, and Block Island, lists 289 species, practically all the species that are found in Rhode Island. Wading birds that have been seen at Ninigret Pond include the snowy egret, glossy ibis, great blue heron, green heron, and black-crowned night heron. In addition, many songbirds frequent the wooded areas of the refuge.

Forty species of mammals have been recorded, including red and gray foxes, coyotes, woodchucks, white-tailed deer, and chipmunks.

Camping is available in three areas. Within Ninigret Conservation Area, located in two primitive areas with access by sand trail requiring four-wheel drive, you'll find 20 sites for self-contained units only. The Charlestown Breachway has 75 sites for self-contained trailer units only. You can also camp in the nearby Burlingame State Park in Charlestown. This 3,100-acre park and management area, with frontage on the shore of Watchaug Pond, has a large camping area with 730 sites. Facilities include tables, fireplaces, and rest rooms with showers.

Those interested in nature will find that Burlingame State Park is an excellent area for seeing birds and other wildlife, especially during the quieter spring and fall months (before hunting season begins). As many as 80 species of birds nest in Burlingame, and even more species can be seen during migration periods in the winter. In recent years, Watchaug Pond has been noted as a place to look for wintering bald eagles. Species that nest in Burlingame include wood ducks, broad-winged hawks, great horned owls, great crested flycatchers, hermit thrushes, cedar waxwings, red-eyed vireos, and scarlet tanagers.

Mammals that inhabit the park include white-tailed deer, eastern cottontail rabbits, red and gray squirrels, muskrats, mink, raccoons, red foxes, river otters, and even short-tailed weasels.

In early spring, the call of male wood frogs sounds like the quacking of ducks, but perhaps the sound most associated with the arrival of spring is the evening chorus of spring peepers. In moist, wooded areas, redback and spotted salamanders find shelter under rocks and decaying logs, while in summer, you may come upon an eastern box turtle hunting beetles or feeding on wild berries. Harmless snakes, including the northern water snake and eastern garter snake, are also found at Burlingame.

Where: Ninigret Conservation Area is reached via East Beach Road, off U.S. 1 in Charlestown.

Ninigret Park is off State 1A in Charlestown.

The entrance to Burlingame State Park is on U.S. 1 in Charlestown.

Charlestown Breachway is off Charlestown Beach Road in Charlestown.

Hours: Ninigret Conservation Area and Ninigret Park are open daily, year-round, from sunrise to sunset. Camping is available in Ninigret Conservation Area, and the Charlestown

Breachway from April 15 to October 31. Burlingame State Park is open for camping from April 15 to October 1.

Admission: A fee is charged for parking at Ninigret Conservation Area daily during the summer season, but weekends and holidays only during the off-season. There is a camping fee at each of the three areas.

Best time to visit: Spring and fall to hike the beach and trails. The area is crowded in summer.

Activities: At Ninigret Conservation Area, there is hiking, wildlife watching, swimming (lifeguard on duty 10:00 A.M. to 6:00 P.M. during the summer), boating, fishing, and shellfishing (nonresident license required).

At Burlingame State Park, there is camping, boating, fishing, and swimming in Watchaug Pond. Also hiking, birding, other wildlife watching, and photography.

The Charlestown Breachway offers camping, a boat-launching ramp, saltwater fishing, and swimming.

The Frosty Drew Memorial Nature Center in Ninigret Park has nature trails, an observatory, interpretive displays, and programs.

Concessions: None.

Pets: Not allowed.

For more information: Rhode Island Department of Environmental Management, Division of Parks and Recreation, 2321 Hartford Avenue, Johnston, RI 02919-1713. Call 401-222-2632.

Ninigret Conservation Area, call 401-322-0450 (seasonal).

Burlingame State Park, call 401-322-7994 or 401-322-7337. (Year-round call 401-322-8910; fax 401-322-3083.)

Charlestown Breachway, call 401-364-7000 (seasonal) or 401-322-8910.

Ninigret Park, call 401-364-1222.

Ninigret National Wildlife Refuge, Box 307, Charlestown, RI 02813. Call 401-364-9124.

Trustom Pond

The Trustom Pond Refuge, part of the Ninigret National Wildlife Refuge, was created when Ann Kenyon Morse donated her 350-acre coastal farm in South Kingston to the U.S. Fish and Wildlife Service in 1974. Today, the refuge includes more than 640 acres of wildlife habitats including fields, shrubs, woodlands, fresh and saltwater ponds as well as sandy beaches and dunes. The refuge is home to some 300 species of birds and more than 40 species of mammals as well as 20 species of reptiles and amphibians. Trustom Pond, Rhode Island's largest protected coastal pond, attracts a great variety of birds and waterfowl that follow the Atlantic Flyway during spring and fall migrations. The shallow body of water surrounded by fields and scrub forest, with abundant berries and fruit from old orchards, provides a plentiful supply of food for wild creatures.

A barrier beach forms the refuge's southern boundary and provides nesting sites for two species of special concern—least terns and piping plovers.

The farm's former barn has been converted into refuge headquarters, and it's a good idea to stop here and pick up a trail map before hiking the circular trail, which offers good observation points on Trustom Pond.

In summer, you will find catbirds, robins, orioles, and thrashers feeding on wild cherries, blueberries, wild grapes, and blackberries. The trail leads to one of the narrow necks that extend into the pond. From this vantage point, you are likely to see the pond's resident flock of mute swans. Especially during spring and fall migrations, you may observe Canada geese, gulls, terns, loons, grebes, and ducks in Trustom Pond. In summer, visitors often spot egrets, herons, ospreys, and cormorants. The opposite shore of the pond is owned by the Rhode Island Audubon Society.

In winter, you can follow the trails on cross-country skis or snowshoes. Horned larks are often seen during the winter months. Such unusual species as murres, dovekies, shearwaters, and guillemots are sometimes blown into the area by coastal storms. You can also search for the tracks of the refuge's mammal population, which includes deer, red and gray foxes, and coyotes.

Where: Follow U.S. 1 north from Charlestown to Moonstone Beach Road exit. Follow the road one mile and turn right on Matunuck School House Road. The entrance to the refuge is 0.7 mile on the left.

Hours: The refuge is open daily, year-round, from sunrise to sunset. However, Moonstone Beach is closed from April 1 to September 15 due to nesting shore birds.

Admission: No charge.

Best time to visit: Spring, fall, and winter.

Activities: Bird-watching, photography, hiking, interpretive walks in summer. Cross-country skiing in winter. Trustom Pond and the acreage owned by the Rhode Island Audubon Society are jointly managed. Naturalists are on hand during the summer months to assist visitors and lead groups on nature walks.

Concessions: None.

Pets: Not allowed.

For more information: Ninigret National Wildlife Refuge, Box 307, Charlestown, RI 02813. Call 401-364-9124.

Beavertail State Park and Conanicut Island

Beavertail State Park is located in the southwestern part of Conanicut Island at the tip of a nine-mile-long strip of land known as "the Beaver," which extends northward into Narragansett Bay from Rhode Island Sound. This beaver-shaped strip of land is connected to the main part of the island by a narrow neck of land at Mackerel Cove, where there is a small sand beach.

Conanicut Island, which you can reach by bridge from the mainland, was once the summer campground of the Narragansett Indians, who sold the island to settlers in 1657. Most of the early settlers were English Quakers, who were sheep farmers. Jamestown has been a summer colony since 1872, and many of the island's early Victorian summer homes are still in use.

A drive along North Road to Conanicut Point takes you past the Jamestown Windmill, which has been restored by the Jamestown Historical Society. Built in 1787 to grind corn, the mill was in operation until 1896. North Road, which follows an old Indian trail, was so named because on a clear night the North Star shines directly above the center of the road. Guided by its light, an Indian could easily travel the length of the island. At the northern tip of the island at Conanicut Point, stop to admire the view of Narragansett Bay and the Rhode Island coast.

Most of the land accessible for hiking, bicycle riding, or camping is located in the part of Conanicut Island that is south of Jamestown. Beavertail State Park encompasses 170 acres of land at the southern tip of the island. The rocky coast at Beavertail is the scenic equal of any spot on the southern New England shore. Fishermen come here in the early morning or evening to cast for striped bass. Others come to watch the surf endlessly breaking on the rocks. Storms launch showers of spray into the air all around the tail of the beaver.

Birdlife as well as marinelife is abundant in this coastal park. As many as 278 species of birds have been recorded on Conanicut Island. The manx shearwater, an oceanic bird usually found way out at sea, was first seen off Beavertail. Deer occasionally swim to the island, and rabbits and skunks are common.

Beavertail State Park is of historical interest because it is the site of Beavertail Lighthouse, the third-oldest continuously operating lighthouse in North America. The first navigational aid at Beavertail dates back to 1705. It consisted of an open-pitch fire built and maintained by local Indians. In 1719, the first fog-warning device was installed. During heavy fog, a cannon was fired at regular intervals. In 1892, a fog bell operated by horses was installed. The present lighthouse dates

Beavertail Lighthouse at Beavertail State Park

back to 1856. Today, it is fully automated with a light that is visible for 17 miles.

Geologic History

This area is of geologic interest because the ledges, composed of hard metamorphic rock, are in contrast to the softer sedimentary rock found in most of the Narragansett basin. During the Ice Age, the sedimentary rock was eroded by the glacier and its meltwater streams, but the hard bedrock was less affected. After the Ice Age ended and the sea level rose, these areas, including Beavertail Point, remained above the water level. Other areas of hard metamorphic rock became the islands of Narragansett Bay. If you examine the rocks, you will find scratches and fractures that were caused by the glacier that moved across New England some 20,000 years ago.

The state-park road circles the point. At intervals, footpaths descend from the parking areas to the rock ledges. Caution is advised when walking on the rock ledges since they can be extremely slippery.

During the winter, the ledges at Beavertail are a good location to see harbor seals, which seek shelter in the protected waters of Narragansett Bay. The best time to look for them is at low tide, when they often rest on the rock ledges. At high tide, they are usually offshore feeding on fish and shellfish. In winter, Beavertail Point is also a likely place to see ducks and geese.

The only camping area on Conanicut Island is in the Fort Getty Recreation Area and is maintained by the town of Jamestown. The recreation area is reached via Fort Getty Road off Beavertail Road, west of Mackerel Cove. The 118 sites, located on Fox Hill, have a panoramic view of Narragansett Bay. In summer, the surrounding meadows are a garden of wild roses, honeysuckle, and deep blue asters. There are 103 sites for trailers with water and electric hookups and a separate tenting area with 15 sites. There is little privacy between sites, but the location and the view are outstanding. Camping permits for all the sites are issued on a first-come, first-served basis. No reservations are taken, and during the summer season there are few vacant sites. Facilities include a boat ramp, a fishing dock, and modern rest rooms with showers. A picnic area on the shore has a covered pavilion, and you can swim at Mackerel Cove beach.

Where: Take State 138 east and south over the Jamestown Bridge to Conanicut Island and Jamestown. To reach Beavertail State Park, take Beavertail Road south from Jamestown about four miles to the park entrance.

Hours: Beavertail State Park is open sunrise to sunset year-round. Beavertail Lighthouse is closed to visitors. However, a pictorial display on the history of lighthouses is located in the assistant lightkeeper's house. Call the museum for times (seasonal 401-423-3270).

The Jamestown Windmill is open from mid-June to mid-September, Saturday and Sunday, 1:00 P.M. to 4:00 P.M., and by appointment.

The camping season at the Fort Getty Recreation Area is May 18 through October 1.

Admission: No charge at Beavertail State Park. Camping fees are charged at the Fort Getty Recreation Area.

Best time to visit: Spring and fall are less crowded. Winter is the time to see harbor seals.

Activities: Fishing, hiking, picnicking, scenic overlooks, naturalist programs, and historic sites. Camping and boating at the Fort Getty Recreation Area, and swimming at Mackerel Cove.

Concessions: None.

Pets: Not allowed in Beavertail State Park. Leashed pets are allowed at Fort Getty Recreation Area.

For more information: Rhode Island Department of Environmental Management, Division of Parks and Recreation, 2321 Hartford Avenue, Johnston, RI 02919-1713. Call 401-222-2632.

For information on Beavertail State Park or Beavertail Lighthouse, write to Goddard Memorial State Park, Ives Road, Warwick, RI 02818. Call 401-884-2010 or 401-423-9941 (seasonal at Beavertail State Park).

Fort Getty Recreation Area, P.O. Box 377, Jamestown, RI 02835. Call 401-423-7211 (year-round).

For additional information on the Jamestown Windmill, contact the Jamestown Historical Society at 401-423-1798.

Prudence Island and the Narragansett Bay National Estuarine Research Reserve

Once part of the Bay Islands Park System, the park on South Prudence Island is now part of the Narragansett Bay National Estuarine Research Reserve (NBNERR), which was created in 1980 to provide stewardship for sensitive estuarine habitat on Prudence, Patience, and Hope Islands. The research reserve includes 2,353 acres of land on the three islands and 1,591 acres of water surrounding the islands out to a depth of 18 feet.

Increased pressures from human activity have had a serious impact on the complex and delicate web of life that exists in Narragansett Bay. Dredging channels, filling wetlands, and polluting the water have all taken their toll on this ecologically fragile area.

Today, federal and state laws are providing some degree of protection from the destructive forces that threaten Narragansett Bay, but it is felt that public appreciation and awareness may well be the most valuable force in the ongoing effort to save this precious natural resource.

To learn more about the reserve, you can visit South Prudence Island. The Prudence Ferry provides daily year-round service (except on Christmas and New Year's Day) from Church Street Wharf in Bristol. The ferry docks at Homestead, in the central part of the island. Since Prudence Island is less than seven miles long, bicycles are ideal for exploring. You can also bring a car to the island, but motor vehicles are permitted on the roads in the South Park section of the reserve only.

South of the ferry landing, on the eastern shore, is the location of the Sandy Point Lighthouse. Built in 1823 on Goat Island, the lighthouse was moved to Prudence Island in 1851. It is the oldest existing lighthouse in Rhode Island.

North Prudence Island has a three-mile-long main trail to the John Brown Farm and excellent birding trails. A four-mile trail follows the shore of South Prudence, and the Prudence Conservancy, a nonprofit land trust dedicated to maintaining the natural beauty and unique character of Prudence Island, maintains an additional six miles of trails.

South Prudence Park has a limited public mooring area for those who come to the island by private boat. The moorings are available for day use only.

Prudence is the only one of the islands that is inhabited. Settled in the 1600s, the central part of the island still has both permanent and seasonal residents. Approximately 150 people spend their winters on Prudence, and in the summer, the population increases to more than 1,500. Still, the hectic pace of modern life hasn't touched this island. Roads are unpaved and visitors can spend the day hiking or bicycling on the network of trails, birding, attending programs at the Learning Center, and swimming (at your own risk).

South Prudence Island has rock cliffs along the waterfront and cobble beaches, including a swimming beach. An extensive eelgrass meadow occupies the southeastern shore.

Reserve facilities include a residence for visiting scientists, a naturalist's kiosk, with an aquarium and displays of beachcombing treasures, and a field station with a learning center, research lab, and reserve offices.

The Learning Center, which is open during the summer months from Friday through Monday, houses a natural history museum with dioramas depicting typical habitats found within the reserve. Many exhibits are designed for children and provide a hands-on learning experience.

The center also houses an aquarium with constantly changing live specimens taken from Narragansett Bay. Outside, visitors will find a butterfly garden, and inside, a collection of preserved butterflies for up-close study. Several species of butterflies are found in the reserve, including the clouded sulpher and the monarch.

The interpretive exhibits are maintained by the Audubon Society of Rhode Island, which also offers educational programs for visitors as well as a schedule of classroom programs. Naturalists conduct tours of the reserve throughout the summer and fall, both on foot and by bicycle. Programs are designed around specific interests, including wetlands, trees, wildflowers, and beachcombing.

Prudence Island has a large area of upland habitat covered with a dense growth of shrubs, including bayberry, blueberry, blackberry, red cedar, pitch pine, and black cherry. In some areas, a deciduous mixed oak forest has replaced the shrub growth. The island provides shelter and food for many species of birds. Look for bright yellow goldfinches and sharp-tailed sparrows. The woods are home to many birds, including towhees, nuthatches, titmice, and chickadee, while swallows frequent the meadowlands. Lucky birders on the island at the right time may see orioles, warblers, and perhaps a scarlet tanager or indigo bunting. Prudence Island is also home to red-tailed hawks, northern harriers, and owls that inhabit the woodland areas and marshes. Least terns have a nesting ground on the northern end of Prudence Island.

Hope Island, with its salt marshes, located 1.5 miles west of Prudence Island, is one of the most important nesting areas for wading birds on the east coast. Blue herons, great egrets, snowy egrets, and black-crowned night herons, all seek food in the quiet, shallow waters. Kingfishers and glossy ibis also reside in the marsh.

During the winter months, reserve beaches are a good place to observe waterfowl, including black ducks, scoters, mergansers, and canvasbacks. In addition, common loons and horned grebes are frequently seen.

Winter is also a good time to observe harbor seals, which can often be spotted at low tide on the rocky ledges on both the northern and southern tips of Prudence Island. Other mammals that may be found in the reserve include white-tailed deer, red foxes, raccoons, eastern cottontail rabbits, and squirrels.

Amphibian species include the rare spotted turtle, a semi-aquatic species found in wet woodlands and meadows. Box turtles, common in the upland areas, can often be seen crossing Prudence Island roads.

Where: Prudence Island can be reached by ferry service from Church Street Wharf in Bristol, Rhode Island. Church Street Wharf is off State Street, two miles north of the Mount Hope Bridge.

Hours: The Narrangansett Bay National Estuarine Research Reserve is open year-round from 6 A.M. until one-half hour after sunset. The Learning Center is open Friday to Monday from Memorial Day through Labor Day from 11:00 A.M. until 3:00 P.M. It is recommended that visitors call 401-683-6780 to confirm these hours, because field work or other planned activities might be in progress during regular visitors' hours.

Admission: No fee is charged for access to the reserve. Contact the Audubon Society of Rhode Island at 401-949-5454 regarding fees for programs and a schedule. Check with the Prudence Ferry for a schedule and rates for transportation to and from the island.

The reserve is divided into three zones in which different restrictions apply. A permit is required from the reserve manager for educational groups of more than 12 people. Hope Island is closed during spring and summer in order not to disturb nesting shore birds.

Best time to visit: Spring and fall (before hunting season) for birding. Summer to visit the Learning Center and participate in its programs. Winter to observe waterfowl and harbor seals.

Activities: Birding, hiking, bicycling, nature observation and photography, picnicking (be sure you leave behind nothing but footprints—littering is strictly forbidden on all reserve properties), swimming (at your own risk), fishing and shellfishing (provided that state laws are obeyed), and seasonal naturalist programs and tours, both on foot and by bicycle.

Concessions: None.

Not allowed: Pets on reserve properties. Camping. Open fires. The removal of plants, wildlife, or anything else—everything on reserve property is an integral part of the environment and is protected. Motorized vehicles on any of the trails.

A word of caution: Beware of ticks that can carry Lyme and other diseases. They are present on Prudence Island. Wear protective clothing and use insect repellent. Also, check for ticks after spending a day outside.

In summer and fall, chiggers may be a problem. These parasites can infest fields and woods and feed on any animal or human. Stay on the trails to avoid these pests.

In addition, keep in mind that hunting is permitted on the reserve during those seasons determined by the Rhode Island Division of Fish and Wildlife. It is best to avoid visiting the reserve during hunting season.

For more information: State of Rhode Island and Providence Plantations, Department of Environmental Management, Narragansett Bay National Estuarine Research Reserve, P.O. Box 151 South Park, Prudence Island, RI 02872. Call 401-683-5061.

Audubon Society of Rhode Island, 12 Sanderson Road (Route 5), Smithfield, RI 02917-2606. Call 401-949-5454.

Prudence Ferry, Inc., Church Street Wharf, Bristol, RI 02809. Call 401-253-9808.

Blithewold Gardens and Arboretum

To experience a place of natural beauty that man has had a hand in creating and preserving, visit Blithewold Gardens and Arboretum in Bristol. Situated on 39 acres along the shore of Narragansett Bay, Blithewold was the 45-room summer home of Augustus Van Winkle, who had made his fortune in the coal industry. Built in 1908, the house and gardens, which include a rose garden, a water garden, and a rock garden, were designed by New York landscape architect John DeWolf.

Marjorie Van Winkle Lyon, daughter of the original owner, spent her summers at Blithewold until her death at the age of 93. During her lifetime, she continued a family tradition of opening Blithewold to horticultural groups during the gardening season, and in her will she bequeathed Blithewold to the Heritage Trust of Rhode Island to ensure that visitors would always be able to enjoy the gardens and special beauty of this turn-of-the-century estate. Today, the mansion, arboretum, and gardens are on the National Register of Historic Places.

In addition to native plants, you will find exotic species not usually found elsewhere in New England. One of these is a Chinese toon tree, the first known to flower in the United States. There is also a 90-foot giant sequoia, planted in 1911, which is the largest of its kind east of the Rocky Mountains. The tree grows about a foot a year. There are also Chinese cedars, ginkgoes, and a grove of bamboo believed to be the largest stand of bamboo in the Northeast. A brochure is available that describes the many species of trees you will see along a self-guided trail. You can also take a guided tour of the grounds and the 17th-century-style English manor house, which is furnished and decorated much as it was in the early 1900s. There is a gift shop in the carriage house. Bring a lunch to enjoy in one of the picnic areas on the lawns overlooking Narragansett Bay.

Where: From Providence, take exit 2 off I-195 in Massachusetts. Follow State 136 south for 8.5 miles. Turn right on Griswold Avenue. At the end of Griswold Avenue, turn left onto Ferry Road (State 114); Blithewold is a quarter-mile on the right.

Hours: The grounds are open year-round, 10:00 A.M. to 5:00 P.M. The mansion is open April 15 to September 30, Tuesday through Sunday, and Monday holidays, 10:00 A.M. to 4:00 P.M. In December, Christmas at Blithewold is celebrated. Call in December for holiday exhibits and hours. The mansion is closed July 4 and December 25. The gift shop is open daily, April to December.

Admission: A fee is charged for admission to the grounds and for tours of the mansion and grounds.

Best time to visit: April for spring bulb display, May through September to see the gardens in bloom.

Activities: Touring the mansion, gardens, arboretum; picnicking and special programs, including Concerts by the Bay (June to September), and horticultural and historical programs throughout the year; also, Christmas at Blithewold in December.

Concessions: None.

Pets: Not allowed.

For more information: Blithewold Gardens and Arboretum, 101 Ferry Road, Bristol, RI 02809-0716. Call 401-253-2707.

Reading Guide

Bolles, Frank. *At the North of Bearcamp Water*. Boston and New York: Houghton Mifflin, 1896.

Borland, Hal. *Beyond Your Doorstep: A Handbook to the Country*. New York: Knopf, 1962.

Bowen, Ezra. "The Million Dollar Fish," *Connecticut Magazine*, May 1994, 39–44.

Burroughs, John. *Birds and Poets*. Vol. 3 of *The Writings of John Burroughs*. 19 vols. Boston and New York: Houghton Mifflin, 1877, 1895, and 1904.

Colbert, Edwin H. *The Great Dinosaur Hunters and Their Discoveries*. New York: Dover Publications, 1984.

Cooley, Susan D. *Country Walks in Connecticut: A Guide to the Nature Conservancy Preserves*. Boston: Appalachian Mountain Club and The Nature Conservancy, 1982.

Devine, Arnold "Buzz," and Dwight G. Smith. *Connecticut Birding Guide*. Dexter, MI: Thomson-Shore, Inc., 1996.

Godin, Alfred J. *Wild Mammals of New England*. Field Guide Edition. Freeport, ME: DeLorme Publishing, 1983.

Hardy, Gerry, and Sue Hardy. *Fifty Hikes in Connecticut*. 3rd ed. Woodstock, VT: Backcountry Publications, 1993.

Hicock, Shelton B., ed. *Connecticut Walk Book*. Middletown: Connecticut Forest and Park Association, 1981.

Hill, Evan. *The Connecticut River*. Photography by William F. Stekl. Middletown: Wesleyan University Press, 1972.

Jaques, Florence Page. *Canoe Country*. (Illustrated by Francis Lee Jacques) Minneapolis: University of Minnesota Press, 1938.

Klemens, Michael W. *Checklist of the Amphibians and Reptiles of Connecticut with Notes on Uncommon Species*. Hartford, CT: Connecticut Department of Environmental Protection, 1991.

Lawrence, Gale. *A Field Guide to the Familiar*. Hanover, NH: University Press of New England, 1998.

Lippincott, Bertram. *Jamestown Sampler*. Ambler, PA: John L. Gaghen & Assoc., 1980.

Mallett, Sandy. *A Year with New England's Birds: A Guide to Twenty-five Field Trips*. Somersworth: New Hampshire Publishing, 1978.

Olson, Sigurd F. *Reflections from the North Country*. New York: Knopf, 1976.

Perry, John, and Jane Greverus Perry. *The Sierra Club Guide to the Natural Areas of New England*. San Francisco: Sierra Club Books, 1990.

Peterson, Roger Tory. *A Field Guide to the Birds*. 2nd rev. & enl. ed. Boston: Houghton Mifflin, 1960.

Proctor, Noble S. *25 Birding Areas in Connecticut*. Chester, CT: Pequot Press, 1978.

Ritchie, David, and Deborah Ritchie. *Connecticut Off the Beaten Path*. Chester, CT: Globe Pequot Press, 1992.

Schroeder, Marion. *Gardening in New England Including New York State: A Resource Guide*. New York: Harper & Row, 1990.

Scull, Theodore. *Water Trips: A Guide to East Coast Cruise Ships, Ferryboats, and Island Excursions*. Camden, ME: International Marine Publishing, 1987.

Sutton, Ann, and Myron Sutton. *Eastern Forests*. Audubon Society Nature Guides. New York: Knopf, 1985.

Sutton, Caroline, ed. *The Audubon Society Field Guide to the Natural Places of the Northeast*. Vol. I, Coastal. New York: Pantheon Books, 1984.

Taylor, Sally L., Glenn D. Dreyer, and William A. Niering. *Native Shrubs for Landscaping*. New London, CT: The Connecticut College Arboretum, 3rd printing, 1992.

Teale, Edwin Way. *A Naturalist Buys an Old Farm*. New York: Dodd, Mead, 1974.

Thoreau, Henry David. *Walden*. New York: Doric Books. Stratford Press, 1950.

Tyning, Thomas F. *A Guide to Amphibians and Reptiles*. Stokes Nature Guides. Boston: Little, Brown, 1990.

Wass, Stan. *25 Ski Tours in Connecticut*. Somersworth: New Hampshire Publishing, 1978.

Weber, Ken. *Canoeing Massachusetts, Rhode Island, and Connecticut*. Woodstock, VT: Backcountry Publications, 1986.

————. *25 Walks in Rhode Island: A Hiker's Guide to Trails from Buck Hill to Block Island*. Somersworth: New Hampshire Publishing, 1978.

Weidensaul, Scott. *Seasonal Guide to the Natural Year: A Month by Month Guide to Natural Events: New England and New York*. Golden, CO: Fulcrum Publishing, 1993.

Wetmore, Alexander. *Song and Garden Birds of North America*. Washington, DC: National Geographic Society, 1964.

Wilson, Alex. *Appalachian Mountain Club Quiet Water Canoe Guide: Massachusetts, Connecticut, Rhode Island: Best Paddling Lakes and Ponds for All Ages*. Boston: Appalachian Mountain Club Books, 1993.

Index